Rise of the Next Wave

THE LEADERSHIP JOURNEY
VOLUME II

Jeff Levitan

Dedication:

To all the people who take responsibility for their futures and commit their lives to helping others, this book was written for you!

TABLE OF CONTENTS

Forward / Special Note:

Have you ever wondered if you were too late to the game to win? You had to be in early to get the good positions or maybe the real opportunity has come and gone. Nothing could be further from the truth! In many businesses today, technology and the speed of innovation have leveled the playing field from the early-comers to the late-comers. Starting later in this era usually means you've only missed the growing pains.

Rise of the Next Wave is a collection of exciting stories from the newest wave of ultra-successful business leaders. As they tell their stories within these pages, you will discover many of the developed skills and habits which are easily understood, but challenging to practice. Rarely will you find such a degree of success from people with such humble beginnings. Their stories will inspire you to reach further and become more. The instruction within these pages will compel you to drive harder, believe more, and most importantly never give up on your dreams!

My wish for you is that you get specific instruction from this book as well as business ideas that may be implemented immediately. Many great businesses are run by what we call a power couple. Fortunately, this book tells multiple sides and perspectives of what it means to win, by the spouses of the great business Heroes. I've heard it said that although it's special to meet a winner, it's rare to meet a winner married to a winner. You will read the stories of many of them in this book. Enjoy reading the Rise of the Next Wave and see yourself being the next great story!

With Hope, Courage, and Faith,

Jeff Levitan

Chapter 1
Rob Day

After 45 years of living on this earth, I have found that, in most cases, things are not as good as they seem up front. They might still be good, but just not as good as they first appeared. There is usually some little disclaimer or catch that diminishes how good the opportunity looked at first glance.

In my life, there have been three exceptions to this rule. The first is my relationship with God, the second is my marriage and family life, and the third is my WFG business. All three of these seemed like beneficial choices in the beginning, but what they have grown into has surpassed all expectations and even all dreams of what I thought they could become.

I am a very blessed man to say the least. As I write, I am with my family vacationing in Sorrento, Italy, and overlooking the Tyrrhenian Sea from our villa in the Bay of Naples. This particular vacation began in London. Then our large group of family and friends took a train to Paris and a day trip to Versailles. In that setting, we were blessed to witness our son, Hunter, propose to a beautiful and Godly young lady named Allyson. We then flew to Rome with a group of church leaders to spend Pentecost with our international members from around Europe. From there, we were off to Tuscany, where we witnessed our daughter, Madison, become engaged to a Godly young man named Christian. The setting for this memorable event was a field of fireflies on the grounds of a historic vineyard and villa where we all spent several days. From there, we drove down to Sorrento, Italy, were we are staying in a villa up on a cliff overlooking the Bay of Naples. This has definitely been a once-in-a lifetime trip. That said, our associations with WFG have given us 50 lifetimes worth of once-in-a-lifetime vacations.

When we get home from this three-week vacation in Europe, we will return to a beautiful antebellum home built in 1861. WFG has paid me over $100,000 in a week multiple times this year and my income continues to rise. The decisions we have made when opportunities were presented to us in our faith, family life, and business have created a dream life that is beyond description.

The Keys to My Personal Success

People always want to know the secret of this success. The truth is, there really aren't any secrets because the leaders have been giving them away for over 30 years. The key is that you must apply what you are being taught. After 30 plus years of our business model being run, there are probably millions of notebooks filled with the secrets of our business. Unfortunately, most of those note takers never consistently applied what they learned in those notes. They say that knowledge is power, but what I have learned is that applied knowledge is power.

The first four years of my business were a struggle. There were many reasons for this struggle. But, it basically came down to my willingness to consistently apply the success principles that we are taught in WFG.

There are many keys to success, a few stick out as I reflect on the last twenty-three years. One of the main keys is you must be very careful who you allow to influence your life choices. I was very blessed to associate with great leaders early in my career - men like Rich Thawley, Ed Mylett, Jeff Levitan, and Greg Kapp. Everyone else talked a good game, but I noticed few had actually built a business that looked like what I hoped to build. I quickly learned to tune out the others and focus on listening to those actually achieving the success I was dreaming of attaining myself. It took me a little longer to figure out that I needed to apply this same principle in my marriage and spiritual life.

Spiritual Strength

Today, I surround myself with people who have great marriages and incredible relationships with God. By applying what I have learned from them, I now have a marriage and spiritual life beyond what I thought was possible.

We are surrounded by mediocrity in all of these areas. Conventional wisdom will tell you that you cannot achieve excellence. Thankfully, I ran into people who kept interrupting all of those voices telling me I couldn't do something. These great leaders showed me with their personal examples that I could do it. I mentioned some of the leaders who taught me excellence in business, but I feel compelled to mention those who influenced me to pursue excellence in my marriage and spiritual life. In our marriage, we had Rich and Cindy Thawley, along with our spiritual leaders. In our spiritual life, it was pastor and author Gwen Shamblin that showed us that we could be whole-hearted towards God the way I had been taught to be whole-hearted towards the business.

One of the things that I heard from stage, that I have repeated many times, is that God has to come first, family second, and the business third. This philosophy, that many of the leaders have spoken, was one of the attributes that attracted me to WFG. Unfortunately, I repeated that mantra many times before it was a reality in my life.

I have experienced success both with and without God being my main focus. For me, success was empty in my life without God on his rightful throne. As a matter of fact, the more I achieved the more empty it became. I think the reason for this was that once I began achieving material possessions and accolades, I thought those things would bring happiness outside of God. It became scary to realize that none of these things can really bring true happiness. I had achieved much success in business, but was not happy and at peace until I learned to truly put God ahead of everything else in my life.

Learn and Apply

My business path was motivated by what I saw in the company story and how excited I was about what it could do for my family. I loved that I could have a chance at success while helping people. I, like most, thought that building a business would be much easier then it was and that it would happen much faster than it did. After about four years of struggling, I finally began to apply what I had been taught. The result was an explosion in my business. We rose rapidly through the ranks of WFG from 1998 to 2001. By the end of that time frame, our incredible business model had allowed me to build the foundation for the team that I have today. I worked harder than I ever had in my life during that time and the payoff was a business that continues to grow - whether I do anything or not.

Leading by Example

So that there is no confusion, I had achieved the top position in the company before I slowed down in my personal activity. I held the record for personal and base shop production during my building years. I was taught to lead by example and that is what I did. Only a few leaders in my business have ever surpassed the records I set when I was fully engaged and active. This is one of the biggest mistakes I see up-and-coming leaders make. They slow down their personal activity way too soon then wonder why they don't have a business that perpetually grows with or without them.

There are leaders who have, and will, far exceed my success by staying personally active for a longer period of time than I did. But the minimum time that you must stay active, in my opinion, is until you reach EVC. Odds are, that this is what will give you the basis of a team that will continue to grow. The reason for this is in how our company is structured. When I bring someone into our company, it's not to make them one of my agents. I'm simply handing them their own company. This means that they are empowered to build something for their family that they own. Owners of their own company will go on with or without you. Having an army of independent business owners that are focused on their dreams through building their own businesses is what gives you total freedom of time and finances.

The Most Important Secret to Success

The most important secret I want to give you will, if followed, allow you to learn all of the other secrets in our business. It is something I first heard while listening to Greg Kapp at a company convention. The secret is: "Join and don't quit." The reason this is, in my opinion, the most important secret is because as long as you don't quit, you will eventually find and learn how to apply all of the other secrets.

The only thing that separates me and the other leaders in WFG from all of those who didn't make it, is that they quit and we didn't. We all had different time frames, paths, and experiences on our journey to success. But not quitting is what allowed us to get to where we are today.

Building a Family Business

As I finish writing my chapter of this book inspired by Jeff Levitan, I am on the island of Capri in Italy, sitting next to the love of my life and wife of 25 years. She is holding our first granddaughter, Giselle, and watching our other children swim in the sea. My oldest daughter, Lacy, and her husband, Jay, are SMDs and soon to be EMDs. Our other two oldest children, Hunter and Madison, are entering into the business. They already have a great start and I'm very proud of them.

I think one of the biggest testaments to our business is that our children want to join it and that I allow them to. From my perspective, if I didn't have a moral foundation in my life, I might be the type of person willing to tell you that this is a great business, even if I didn't truly believe it, but I wouldn't expose my kids to it. From my kids' perspective, they grew up behind the scenes. They know whether the incredible life we talk about is true or not. They have lived it. So, for me or any leader to be willing to bring our children into the business, or for our children to want to join the business after growing up in it, speaks volumes.

God has truly led us on a path to a dream life. We are very grateful and give all credit for anything good in our lives to Him.

CHAPTER 1
ROB DAY

Chapter 2
Fradel Barber

How does a shy, 20-year-old kid from Brooklyn go out on her own to Los Angeles, California, and build a business in a field she knows nothing about? The odds of being success are not in favor. Yet, that kid found an organization that would help her build a business that was profitable year over year. That organization was World Financial Group, and that kid was me.

A great mentor of mine, Gregg Kapp, told me very early on in my career, "Know what you know. Know what you don't know. And know who knows what you don't know. That's all you need to know!"

When I started out in this business, I knew there were many things I didn't know. I didn't know anything about financial services, I didn't have a college degree, and I came from a creative field with a complete right-brained thought process. On paper, I didn't stand a chance.

The story of how I came to be an entrepreneur who leverages the World Financial Group platform is one of struggle, faith, risk, and, most of all, perseverance. Fortunately, while we are all unique in our own way, there are many lessons we can learn from one another which will help us along our journeys throughout life and building our businesses.

I was raised in Brooklyn, New York, as the eldest of 12 children born to Jewish, Ultra-Orthodox, Hassidic parents. Growing up in a ghetto-like environment kept me secluded and insulated from a world filled with opportunity. Orthodox Jewish girls in our community were expected finish high school, learn additional Hebrew studies for one year, and then get set up to be married and have as many children as possible. College wasn't encouraged or planned for, and a career was out of the picture.

While I acknowledged the blessings associated with that type of lifestyle, I always found myself wanting more. As early as I can remember, I wanted to see more, do more, and be more. At the age of 16, a friend and I started a business that offered design services such as logos, flyers, and brochures. Our initial success got me really excited. But then the realities of being young, inexperienced, and broke set in. Our equipment, which we saved up every last penny to buy, broke down. We weren't completing projects on time. And we started losing the first few clients we had.

Although my first business venture was a failure, I was determined to succeed. So, I tried another avenue of design that intrigued me - jewelry. Once again, business wasn't what I thought it would be and I learned that running a business was different than having a skill and utilizing it to be self-employed.

At that time, I jumped at an opportunity to study abroad. I was finally able to leave my parents nest, and the secluded community that I grew up in, to travel the world. I returned to America a year later with a new-found appreciation for our country, our freedom, and our capitalist society. And with my mind set on leaving the freezing winters and dirty subways of New York, I quickly imagined the perfect place to relocate: beautiful and sunny Los Angeles.

Once the decision was made, I went all out to make it happen – fast. I planned everything out to the last detail. I set up a bunch of interviews for when I got to Los Angeles so I could have a job lined up, I registered at a local design college so I could continue my studies, and I even arranged for a car to be purchased and ready for me when I stepped off the plane. Although I didn't know anyone in LA, I managed to find a temporary place to stay for three months while I got settled. Everything was thought out and pre-planned.

As I touched down in LA and felt the sun and the cool breeze, I thought I had made it. But, as they say, "Man plans and God laughs." My plans must have been the biggest joke of the century, because outside of those first few days of taking it all in, everything I planned went up in smoke.

Of the 10 interviews I had set up, I didn't land even one second interview. My savings were running out very quickly, and the time I had left to stay at the temporary housing was coming to an end. Worst of all, I had never owned a car before and was ignorant on the need to put oil in a used car. Within two months, all of my hard-earned savings blew up with the engine. I found myself homeless, jobless, penniless, and carless. It seemed like the only thing that worked out was my college registration. I was registered and pre-paid for my first semester, which was scheduled to start in three weeks.

I have to admit, I briefly considered going back to New York. I wondered: Should I call it quits and go back home? Should I just throw in the towel and give up on all my dreams? That dialogue played in my head for a brief moment before I reminded myself that there was no way that was going to happen and I was going to make it. I had one last interview scheduled and I prayed it was "the one."

That last interview was the first day I walked into a World Financial Group office. As I sat down and had the business presented to me by Elan Michael, I was very skeptical and didn't "get it." I didn't understand anything regarding the financial part of the business, how it worked, and, most of all, how I would get clients. However, I did grasp the value of aligning with a mentor who was already successful and would guide me with everything I needed to achieve success. A mentor was something I felt was missing in everything else I had tried up until that point. That certainly intrigued me. Yet, I still wasn't ready to make a decision and walked out of the meeting telling Elan that I would think about it. He later told me he thought I would never come back.

After meeting with Elan again the next day, I still wasn't ready to make a decision because I was concerned about how I was going to get clients, considering I was new to LA and didn't know anyone. Elan then invited me to come back the following day to a corporate overview where I would get to meet his business partners. I agreed, as I figured this would be a way for me to find out more about how to get clients.

When I came back the next day and entered the BPM (Business Presentation Meeting) room, I saw a bunch of professional-looking men and women and was immediately overwhelmed. Being very shy, I felt uncomfortable in a room full of people that I didn't know. But, I didn't feel that way for long, because someone immediately walked over to me, offered an introduction, and took a genuine interest in me. Each person I met proceeded to edify and tell me great things about Elan. I immediately felt fortunate to be in the presence of such a great group of people and so lucky to be trained by Elan, the top person in the company!

I asked each person who was introduced to me, "How do you get your clients?" The answers I got were shocking and irritating at the same time. They referenced the system, which is what Elan had told me the day before. At the very end of what I later learned was the Mo-zone (Momentum Zone), I met this guy named Art. He was from New York and had the attitude to match, which made me feel at home. When I asked him my client question, he looked me in the eyes and told me very directly, "No one in this room tonight is going to tell you how we get our clients. Why should they? It's our trade secret. However, what I will tell you is that if you follow that system, you will never have a problem finding clients."

I don't know if it was the New York in him, or the direct way in which he said it, but it was at that moment that I made my decision to join WFG. And the rest is history!

The Keys to My Personal Success

What is it that makes someone extraordinary? Is it a title? Is it a degree? Is it luck? Is it genetics? In most cases, it's none of these! When you take a look at people who are extraordinarily successful in any given area, you can see many commonalities in their actions and mindset.

I've been blessed to be surrounded by many extraordinary people in my 11 years as an entrepreneur, from millionaires, to extraordinary communicators, to successful entrepreneurs, to people with the greatest physiques. While getting to know their stories and how they got to where they currently are, I've come to recognize 10 points that many of them have in common. These are things I applied in my personal life and continue to improve upon every day.

1. Passion. In order to achieve something great, you have to be passionate about what you are doing. This doesn't mean every day will be perfect, or that you won't have to do

some things you don't love to do. Instead, it means that you do everything with passion and love what you do. When I started my business with World Financial Group, I was so passionate about it that you couldn't get me to talk about anything else. Any entrepreneur that is extraordinary will live and breathe their business because they are passionate about it. That passion drives them.

2. Decisiveness. It all starts with a decision. Don't attempt to "try" things. Decide that you are going to do something and then go all out and do it. Have a "do or die" mentality If it doesn't work, learn from your failures. The saying "never burn your bridges" should only be applied to relationships and connections with people, not as a safety net to prevent you from fully committing to something you want to do.

I remember the day I truly decided to become a full-time entrepreneur with WFG. Just two weeks after starting with WFG, I was prepared to face my first day of classes at the design college. I started out in the early morning for a long commute through heavy traffic. As I sat on the freeway, which looked more like a parking lot, I began to wonder why I was going to school. My original plan was to gain knowledge and to be able to get an opportunity. It then occurred to me that I already had an opportunity. At that point, I made one of the biggest and best decisions of my life. I decided to quit school and work on my business full time. At that very moment, I exited the freeway and headed to the office to start that journey. Needless to say, that decision and the actions that followed changed my life!

3. Action. Measure your expectations according to your actions. You won't get a different result from doing the same thing you've always done. If you intend to change something in your life or in your business, then you need to change what you are doing. Sometimes it's easy to get caught up in daily activities that keep us busy, although they are not actions that will make our business grow. One thing I always make sure to do is measure the actions that are being done on

a daily basis that are directly correlated to results in my business, such as prospecting, setting appointments, and doing appointments.

"There are risks and costs to action. But they are far less than the long-range risks of comfortable inaction." - John F. Kennedy

4. Growth. Never stop growing. You're always either growing or dying. Growth is not always comfortable or convenient. You can be comfortable or extraordinary, but not both. Personal development is a key factor in any successful endeavor. As you grow, it's important to seek out mentors and people who are better than you in the areas you want to improve. I believe that personal mentors are invaluable and should not be taken for granted. Earn the time you spend with them, and thank them by doing what they are guiding you to do.

I remember the first time I met my mentor, Greg Kapp, at a big event. After receiving an award for being the number one personal recruiter, I asked him what I needed to do to be able to receive his mentorship. I followed the set of instructions he gave me - exactly. I felt I had earned the right to request him to mentor me because of the accomplishment I had already achieved and I made sure I didn't waste his time. I began applying his advice immediately. I believe this was the edge I had over people twice my age. I may have been young and inexperienced, but I always made sure to be the most coachable person in the room. I understood that because of the WFG system, if my trainer was telling me to do it a certain way, which had a proven track record and was part of the system, it was in my best interest to do it exactly that way, as fast as possible, in order to have the fastest and largest growth.

5. Positivity. Be positive, always. Most people have a negative opinion on just about everything and have been programmed that way from a very young age. Being positive not only makes things easier when things don't go right, but it also

makes it more probable for things to go your way. In WFG, we are in the business of attracting people. Having a positive attitude is key.

6. Responsibility. It's easy to put blame on other people or circumstances. But that's what ordinary people do. To be extraordinary, step up and take responsibility for everything in your life. In growing my business, there were many times that things didn't go as planned. I could have blamed the company, the system, the leadership, the economy, the team, etc. Instead, I took responsibility and kept doing the actions that were needed to get it done. At the end of the day, blaming people still won't help you accomplish your goals. Take responsibility and just do it!

7. Determination. It's ok to fail if you give it everything you've got. It's not our successes that make us, it's our failures. Getting back up after being knocked down teaches us so much more. I had many successes throughout my years in WFG. But the moments that were the most memorable and had the biggest impact on me were the ones which were most challenging. When I moved back to New York to expand on the east coast, I thought I had it all figured out. It didn't turn out that way, and many challenges and obstacles got in my way. However, that didn't stop me. I worked and worked until it got done. To this day, opening my New York office is one of my greatest accomplishments.

8. Proactivity. Time is the hottest commodity we have. We don't know how much we have left, and there is nowhere we can purchase more. Don't overthink or over-plan. You get further ahead by taking the plunge and doing it. Adjustments can be made along the way. Ordinary people are constantly thinking about what they want to do. Extraordinary people recognize an opportunity and start immediately, regardless of if they know everything. You won't recognize success without starting. Your mentors in the business will give you a system to follow with a proven method on how to succeed. Don't wait until you know everything to get started. Step-by-step,

just follow the system and you will gain the knowledge through your actions.

"You don't have to see the whole staircase. Just take the first step." – Martin Luther Kind, Jr.

9. Tenacity. Do what needs to be done, regardless of your circumstances. Ordinary people do things based on how they feel. The extraordinary get things done no matter what. Regardless of their emotions, circumstances, or challenges they face, they will make it happen. Life happens, deal with it. Any reason is an excuse. Extraordinary people don't use excuses as to why they can't do things. In New York, we face bad weather and snow storms. One particular winter, there was a big snow storm on a BPM night. Many guests and associates were calling in to cancel their attendance, but I refused to cancel the event. That night, we ended up with me, one other associate, and two guests. One of those guests is now a Senior Marketing Director and a great leader in my organization. You can make excuses or money, but you can't make both.

10. High Standards. Ordinary people tend to wing it and go for bare minimum results when it comes to performance. They accept most anyone into their circle of influence as long as it makes them feel comfortable. Extraordinary people have high standards for themselves, as well as the people they associate with. They guard their associations and have high standards for their own performance, through intense preparation and hard work. This has been one of the biggest things that I changed when I started my business. I completely changed my associations and raised my standards. It is said: "You are equal to the total of the top five people you surround yourself with." Associations don't only mean people you hang out with, but also the things you read, listen to, and watch. I surround myself with ultra-successful people all the time by reading books and listening to audios of people that I want to emulate. This taught me how to raise the standards and

expectations I had for myself and those around me. Setting high standards increases your value.

My Advice to a New Associate

Humans are creatures of habit, not of resolutions. When starting something new, such as your WFG business, you can't expect all your bad habits to disappear and good ones to appear without intentional actions to make it happen. Many times, when people start in WFG, they buy into the dream of what they can accomplish here, but they don't buy into what it takes to get it done. Therefore, you must have an action plan, backed by strong reasons of why you must get it done, in order to fuel the plan.

Every year, during the week between Christmas and the New Year, I work on an intense business and life plan for the upcoming year. I assess the previous year, including what I did and did not get done. I write out my accomplishments and search to see how I have grown as a person. I look to see what habits I need to change so that I can accomplish anything I set out to do in the coming year. I believe that having resolutions or goals without changing your habits is only wishful thinking. If we truly want to stick with our goals, we need to understand that our nature is to do things with a consistent routine which we are used to and to do what feels comfortable. But being content doesn't get us ahead. To continue progressing, we need hope and that is sparked by having big goals and dreams.

"If you're bored with life – you don't get up every morning with a burning desire to do things – you don't have enough goals." – Lou Holtz

Your dream should not be solely monetary. Money is not the end; it is only a means to an end. For example, if you wanted to drill a hole in your wall, you would start with a drill. But, the drill isn't what you really want. You want the hole and you are just using the drill to get it. The hole represents your lifestyle and dreams. The drill represents money, which is the tool you need in order to get it. To accomplish our dreams, we need to establish a deadline. As we know, life happens. There is never a good time to start working on your goals. The only good time is now.

There are a variety of things that can stop us from reaching our goals. For some, it may be their associations and the people they hang around with. For others, it might be watching too much TV instead of reading books. Whatever it is for you, identify the scenarios that cause you to get back into your comfort zone and come up with alternative things you can do when you get into those situations. Be ready for the challenge and know what you are willing to do to make things happen, no matter what comes in your way. Accomplishing your goals and dreams is a journey. More than the things you will accomplish, it's who you become in the process of hitting your goals that makes it so worth it. Once you have all your plans in place and get to work, it is the greatest feeling in the world. You will know exactly where you are, where you are going, and what you need to do to get there. Then, it's just up to you to make it happen. A real decision is measured by the action you take.

"Discipline is the bridge between goals and accomplishment." – Jim Rohn

My Advice to a Leader Who Is Stuck In a Rut

In my first year of starting my business with WFG, at 21 years old, I hit a significant milestone of making a six-figure income and was rewarded not only with money in my bank account, but also with a huge super bowl ring that signified that momentous number. For me, at that age, having started with no market, no experience in the financial industry, and having never made more than $22,000 per year before, it was a great accomplishment. In fact, it was the very reason why I started my business. I knew I wanted to make money, and lots of it. And I had a very clear definition of what lots of money was: $100,000. I laid my plans out carefully of how I was going to do it, and then I did it.

Cash flowing over $100,000 in my first year in business was a big deal to me. But that quickly got old. A couple of years went by and, even though my income kept increasing, making that six-figure income didn't seem as significant. There I was in my early 20s, making great money and living the American dream out in Los Angeles, yet it just didn't feel that great. The very reason I had started in the first place wasn't motivating me anymore, and it was quite disturbing.

It wasn't until my fourth year in business that I had a sudden shift. It came when I heard a talk by Executive Chairman Ed Mylett at a World Financial Group Convention of Champions in Las Vegas. He spoke of how a life was impacted by doing what we do for families. As he gave his speech, he didn't talk about what we do or how, but why we do what we do. Something suddenly clicked. I never talked to people about the "why," because it was never even in my radar. I had always focused on what we did and how we did it and the income it would produce. My only "why" was the bottom line – money. I then recognized that because I had already accomplished my goal of making six figures, I needed to find something beyond just earning money as my "why." I felt completely transformed!

I also knew I had a large task ahead of me, which was figuring out my new "why." This was a process of months of searching within and asking myself lots of deep questions about what I really cared about and what I wanted my legacy to be. I pictured my eulogy and what people would remember about me. I developed my personal mission statement.

I also finally understood that this was a lifelong process and not an overnight transformation. It was a process of constantly developing into a better person, no matter what stage I was at, and I strive to do that on a daily basis. This process is what ultimately prompted me to pick up from where I had built my business in California to go open an office and expand in New York. Many people had told me that I was crazy and it couldn't be done, but I was determined

CHAPTER 2
FRADEL BARBER

to do it. I realized my passion for helping people take control of their finances and for helping people become entrepreneurs and leaders. These were my real "whys." Once I implemented those changes in both my thoughts and in the way I communicated about my business, great things began to happen. I had a strong mission that people were buying into. The people I was attracting to my business were people who shared those values. I was able to open a new office in one of the greatest and most challenging cities in the world, and double my income. And the best part was, it all had a purpose.

If you feel empty about what you do on a daily basis, figure out your why. Make it a priority to search within yourself to understand what makes you feel fulfilled, beyond just money. We only have one life to live. Time is our most valuable asset. We don't know how much we have left and we can't purchase more of it. Make it count.

Common Mistakes Associates Make

One item that I had on my bucket list and a goal that I set for myself to accomplish before I turned 30 was learning how to ride a motorcycle and getting my motorcycle license. The feeling of going fast in the open air has always excited and thrilled me and, at the age of 29, I was legally able to do it.

As I was going through the course to get licensed, there were things I learned that can be identified in every aspect of life. When you are on the bike, the number one thing you must do is look ahead in the direction of where you are headed, as opposed to looking down to see where you are. This is even more important when making a turn and changing direction. If you don't look in the direction you are turning, you won't complete the turn and you will get off track and drop your bike.

Similarly, in life, if you focus on your current circumstances instead of where you are headed, you will fall. It's very easy to get caught up in the day-to-day challenges and adversity that we face. Many times, we over-think things, which causes us to slow down.

In this business, a new associate can get caught up in their current circumstances, lack of knowledge, or lack of experience. To make a change for the better, they must be 100% coachable and be willing to adapt to the system. For someone more seasoned in the business, the biggest mistake they can make is getting satisfied with where they are and forgetting to do the things they did to get there.

Just like driving a motorcycle, you must look ahead to where you are going and not where you are currently positioned. Don't over-think things, just swerve around your challenges and keep moving forward. Understand that it's not just your final destination that counts, but the journey along the way. Keep the focus on where you are headed and enjoy the ride.

Personal Challenges I Had to Overcome

Building a business in a new industry will bring many challenges for anyone and I had more than my fair share. I was 20 years old when I got started, I didn't have support from my family and friends, I didn't have a financial education, I didn't have business or work experience, I didn't have money, I didn't have a job, and I didn't have a place to live. I didn't even know anyone in the area where I was building my business. The only people I did know were either in other places or they were too young. I was in the wrong market, I was extremely shy, and the list goes on. But of all the challenges that I went through and overcame, the biggest for me was building leaders. One of my main reasons for being in WFG was to develop a team of successful leaders that were aligned with my vision, goals, standards, and beliefs. I knew this would bring me the financial security and freedom I desired. Yet, after years of trying, although I was making a multiple six-figure income, I felt like I wasn't getting anywhere toward that goal. Then I learned that leading leaders is different than leading followers. And the only way I could lead a leader was to be worthy of a leader following me. Instead of focusing on changing people, I went about changing myself. In turn, over the next few years, I was able to build a solid group of leaders that I now have the honor of leading and I know there will be many more to come.

Things I Would Do Differently If I Had To Start Over

Looking back at the last 11 years, I wouldn't trade my journey, experiences, and associations for anything. But, if I had to start over again, I would do more of everything and I would do it faster. Have you ever noticed that the busiest and most accomplished people never talk about how busy they are? When you are laser-focused and you completely, obsessively, immerse yourself in your business, you can do so much more than you ever imagined was possible. In building my business, I didn't always have this laser focus. But when I got it, I was able to achieve much more in a shorter amount of time.

Another thing that helps you do more and do it faster is having an immovable deadline. Remember that pre-vacation checklist that you had which was several pages long and it was all due in one day because the next day you were flying out to your destination? How did you manage to get it all done? Having an immovable deadline creates a sense of unparalleled urgency. I learned this very recently in my business, and if I had to start over I would implement this from day one.

For a couple of years, I had been aiming for my CEO promotion. For one reason or another, I kept missing it. Then I found out I was having a baby. Suddenly, I had a deadline that I couldn't move - no matter what. I put together a plan of all the things I needed to accomplish and set about getting it done. In just 90 days I was able to open a 6,000 square foot office on Wall Street in New York City, have five successful grand opening events with a total of over 400 guests, attend Wealth Bowl in Orlando with over 200 associates where we were nominated as MVP, hit my CEO promotion, go to Las Vegas for my first CEO Launch Meeting, hit my $500,000 ring, hit my EVC promotion, promote seven new Senior Marketing Directors and one new Executive Marketing Director, move into a dream apartment on the 30th floor with 180 degree views of New York City, and confidently await the arrival of my son. Who says you can't have your cake and eat it too? We all have the same amount of time in a day; it's all about how you use it!

My Vision for the Future of My Business

In the olden days, the lamplighters of each city would take one torch and go around to light each lamp in the city. From one light, they spread it to everyone and brightened the city. My vision for the future of World Financial Group is that we become like lamplighters. Every person that comes in contact with anyone from WFG, especially from my team, The World Changers, will become better than they were before, in some area of their life. My personal mission statement is: "To have an impact on the people that I come in contact with that affects them in a positive manner; leading them to do great things in the future that will go on to affect other people for generations to come." Through WFG, I hope to pass that on to the associates I get to work with on a daily basis.

This is a historic moment in time. Everything is aligned for us. I believe we are positioned to truly revolutionize the financial services industry and change the way financial services is distributed to the masses. With continued focus on leaving no family left behind and by providing education and resources to people from all walks of life, World Financial Group and Transamerica Financial Advisors will be the premier household name associated with financial services in America. All the entrepreneurs spearheading and leveraging this time in history with our company's platform will become wealthy beyond their wildest dreams and leave multi-generational legacies. I intend to be at the forefront of this amazing company and its mission. I hope to see you there too.

Chapter 3
Chip Palid

I was born in Detroit, Michigan, as the 12th of 17 children. I have nine sisters and seven brothers. My father, Chester E. Palid, was a hardworking man for his entire life. I was named after my dad, but I've always been called Chip. At the time of my birth, my dad was working for Ford Motor Company as a budget control director for new projects, like the original 1965 Mustang. My mom, Madeleine, had her own career as a registered nurse. While raising her children, she managed to take occasional shifts to supplement the family budget.

My dad was the son of Polish immigrants who arrived in this great country through Ellis Island. His family lived through the Great Depression, doing whatever they could to survive. Grandpa Palid worked in the coal mines of Pennsylvania, was a butcher, worked in grocery stores, and did whatever it took to make it in America. Making money, living frugally, and many similar financial life lessons created the foundation for my life. My mother's family originated from Paris, France, and came to America to help settle the French Colonies east of the Appalachian Mountains. Some of her family members were the original settlers of Fort Detroit, at the time just a little outpost on a river in Michigan.

People always ask me, "How did your parents do it?" Well, both of my parents were great leaders. They challenged their kids to exhibit leadership skills at a young age. Everyone always helped out to the best of their abilities. In reality, the more kids you have, the easier it can be. The older kids always helped the younger kids. There was always someone to cook, clean, babysit, run errands, etc. My older sister, Mary Palid Olson, was the ninth born in our family. She is Eric Olson's mother. And as number twelve in the lineup, I am very happy that my parents didn't stop at 11 children.

I believe that coming from a large family prepared me for running a big base shop. I think that an early fear of some agents coming into our company is that if they grow too big and too fast, they may not be able to handle it. The exact opposite is true. All of the leaders in your base shop, essentially all of your SMDs in training, contribute to the success of your base shop. This, in turn, takes a huge load off of you. So fear not, just build it big, and build it fast. I was born into a big base shop. My parents went 17 wide. That's duplication at its finest.

When I was three years old, the Palids moved into an old mansion in the wealthy Palmer Woods neighborhood of Detroit. We were not wealthy by any means; we just needed a house big enough for the 14 children with three more to come. The three-story home was more than 5,000 square feet with a full basement. It was on a half-acre lot with a long driveway, huge lawn, and dozens of mature trees.

My business partner growing up was my brother, Paul. We shoveled, raked, and mowed ourselves through that neighborhood. We always had money because we were willing to go out and earn it. When I turned 12, I added a paper route to the mix. Delivering the *Detroit News* on a bicycle was fun, until I had to deliver the phonebook-sized Sunday editions or schlep newspapers through the snow.

I remember once asking my dad if I could have a new pair of tennis shoes. He responded, "Go look in the box in the basement first." In a big family, there are always items that have plenty of wear left in them, but are just too small for the original owner. My dad's experience of living through the Great Depression and raising so many children taught me to use all of my resources available to the fullest potential, and only go out and buy new if there is no other option. The other not-so-subtle message from my father was that if I really wanted new, I could probably go out and find a way to earn enough and buy it myself. The most valuable lesson my dad taught me was that a good way of contributing to our big family was by being as self-sufficient as possible.

In the 70s, my dad developed a lung condition that flared up in the cold, hard winters of Michigan. His doctor told him to move to a warm, dry climate, or die sooner than he would like. This was also a time when our nation was in a major recession and Michigan was in a full-blown depression. So, right before my 13th birthday, our family, including the half of the kids who still lived at home, loaded up the station wagon and moved to California.

It was hard for me to adjust. There was no snow to shovel, no leaves to rake, and the tiny yards made it hard to make money mowing lawns. My first real job, the kind you had to apply for, was at Winchell's Donut House. It was a great way to make money during my freshman year at Bellarmine College Prep in San Jose. My first boss taught me so much that I am still appreciative of to this day. Very early on, he recognized my "I can do anything" attitude and moved me from the counter to the kitchen. He taught me to mix recipes, bake, cook, decorate pastries, maintain equipment, and how to clean a kitchen - the proper way. Many of my early management skills, both what to do and what not to do, came from my experience at Winchell's. My boss once told me that one day I would be a great leader. That always stuck with me. Words can have a powerful effect on a young man.

There were many times during my teenage years that my friends were at the beach, going to concerts, and just generally having fun, while I was pulling an extra shift somewhere to make ends meet. Sure, that may have bothered me for a quick minute. Yet, I had the pride in knowing that I was self-sufficient and self-supporting while most of them were not at that point.

After high school, I moved to Santa Barbara, enrolled in college, and had some minor sales jobs. I found out that selling was fun, I liked it, and I was pretty good at it. The money wasn't as good as I had hoped, so I took a job delivering parts for a Chevrolet dealership. After a few months of making a little more money, but still not enough to live on in Santa Barbara, I applied for a job on the sales floor of a car dealership. The manager saw a young kid in blue jeans, greasy from delivering parts all day, and quickly turned me down. The rejection only fueled my fire! It was also a good lesson on the importance of making a good first impression. He had no idea who he was saying "no" to. He hadn't really interviewed me, didn't know who I was, had no idea where I came from, and certainly didn't understand my capabilities. So, I put on a suit and tie, went across town to another dealership, and got hired on the spot. In Santa Barbara, I learned a lot about presenting, selling, merchandising, and working for both good and bad managers. I also sold many different product lines and learned a lot about working with people and developing people skills.

Santa Barbara is also where Linda and I met, fell in love, and got engaged. At the time, I was 22 and making good money.

Yet, I had a feeling that if I could do well in a small town, I could do much better in a bigger market. So, we packed up and moved to San Diego, and never looked back.

Linda and I have now been married for over 30 wonderful years. We have been blessed with two incredible children. Our daughter, Emily, recently graduated from The University of Notre Dame, and our son, Casey, is currently playing college football.

Getting to share your life with the person of your dreams and growing a family together has got to be the biggest blessings God can give to a person. It can also be one of the strongest driving motivators for being successful in business and in life.

One of the things I liked about the auto industry was that I could literally move anywhere in the United States and have a way to make a living. Businesses were always looking for good salespeople, and I knew I was good. What most salespeople were earning had no bearing on my likelihood of success. I just had to hear what the "Top Two" were earning and I knew that within 60 days, I would be one of the top earners. All that mattered was that good money was being paid out to the best people who were willing to be focused and willing to put in the effort necessary to get the job done. And one thing that I always prided myself in was consistently making more money than the year before. I have done this ever since I could lift a shovel. These were also some of the main things that attracted me to WFG. There were so many agents that were not only making a good living, but actually making more money than they had ever dreamed possible. That really astonished me. There is also an opportunity to go anywhere in the United States and open a new market. The need for what we do is so great everywhere.

My first job when we arrived in San Diego was selling Nissan cars and trucks. I followed a friend of mine to a Ford dealership in San Diego, which was one of the biggest dealerships in the country. Within 60 days, I was one of the top earning salespeople.

Upper management recognized my skills and talent, so I was put in positions of authority. I was one of the youngest dealership managers in the country by my mid-twenties. The owner then sponsored me to go to the NADA Dealer Academy just outside of Washington, D.C. This was where owners sent the next generation to learn how to take over the family business. I was beyond honored to go and I earned a degree in General Dealership Management. That degree meant I was qualified to manage every single department of an entire dealership, and even an entire auto park. I ended up managing for an owner of multiple dealerships in San Diego. I was then recruited to run both a BMW and Mini Cooper dealership, so we had to part ways. In retrospect, it was interesting to me that after spending more than 20 years of my life helping another man build his dream, I was never given a gold watch or a nice ring. In WFG I was awarded a gold watch in the first few months, a beautiful ring in less than a year, and a trip to Hawaii in my first full year.

I was at the top of my game and I was one of the highest-paid managers in the business. But, I had also just about hit the income ceiling in the auto industry. In order for me to continue making more money year after year, and increasing my annual income as I had done my entire life, I would have to buy my own franchise. I could not go any higher, short of owning my own business. Unfortunately, the point of entry was somewhere north of $10 million dollars. I was good, but I didn't have that type of money.

The first time my young nephew, Eric Olson, called to tell me about the business, I was making good money managing a BMW dealership and I was driving nice cars. I wasn't open to an "opportunity." As our system works, Eric was told to create a Top 100 list and he put my name on the list. And every time he called, I was not in need of "keeping my options open," and I politely declined. Eric remained diligent, and these calls went on for over five years.

In Eric's sixth year, things changed. The year 2008 hit everyone hard, including me. Gas prices doubled, real estate crashed, massive amounts of foreclosures were front-page news. Nobody could get a loan, nobody was buying cars, and dealerships were reducing overhead and laying people off. People in my position were being asked to work twice as many hours for one-third the pay. Now, it was time to see what my options were. I had always been a hard-working and fiscally conservative family man. We had always lived within our means and never took on too much debt. We always believed in the American dream, but corporate America had its own vision of how this was supposed to play out. As the economy began its slide, and financial challenges came our way, I realized that it was time to attempt to re-invent myself. Then the phone rang again.

Eric Olson invited me to San Jose. I was astounded! My 27-year-old nephew had built a thriving and prosperous business in just a few short years. I dissected the business model. The deeper I dug, the better it got. It was simple, it was easy, it was duplicatable, and I was intrigued. What astounded me was how many offices were in the San Francisco Bay area, and how many Eric had developed. By comparison, WFG was practically non-existent in San Diego, the 8th largest city in the USA. I wanted to bring this business model to San Diego. I told Eric that I no longer wanted to work for another man, and I wanted my own business. No longer would I exchange the sweat of my labor for a basic salary while making someone else the wealth that allowed them to live in fancy neighborhoods. I was ready to build a big business for me and my family. I felt that I had finally found the platform and the foundation with which to help me achieve this goal.

After spending over 25 years in the auto industry, and successfully providing a nice standard of living for my family, I was about to change careers, professions, and my entire life. The WFG business model and the support of those that successfully navigated this same course before me, gave me the confidence to know that, not only could I do this, but I could potentially do it very well.

With this amazing opportunity in front of me, I was all in. I signed my AMA on August 1, 2009. I passed all of my exams and had my Life, Health, Series 6, and Series 63 before the end of the month. Two weeks later, I opened my first office in Poway, California. At one of the first "Super Saturdays" I attended in San Jose, Eric Olson introduced me as Uncle Chip. From that day forward, everyone in the company has called me Uncle Chip. And I love it. First of all, I am very proud to be Eric Olson's uncle. But more than that, this is truly is a family business. This is a business that you can be happy and proud to grow with every single member of your family, including my other nephew, Michael Cherniawski, from Florida. It is all about the families we help, including our own.

The Keys to My Personal Success

I had been very successful in life, but I had not yet been successful in WFG. So I humbled myself to be 100% coachable to my 27-year-old nephew. It was the best decision I ever made. Ask yourself: How coachable are you? Your numbers will reflect how coachable you really are.

I strongly believe that to be successful, you have to do first what you fear the most. Get the challenges out of the way first and then free yourself up to be productive. One of my favorite Rich Thawley phrases is: "Seek the heat." Too many people will waste days, weeks, months, and sometimes entire years, because they are paralyzed by the "what-ifs" instead of just tackling them and moving forward. Forward momentum is everything. If you are not at least treading water, you are sinking. So, it's time to get moving. As long as you are moving forward, no matter the speed, you are succeeding.

You also have to know that you are going to be successful. This takes all the fear away. How hard would you work if you absolutely knew that you would not fail? With the approach of seeing the end game as a complete success, your confidence will breed additional success.

I have a strong-follow up ethic. The seeds that you plant early on will bring harvest later. Some will sprout next week, some will blossom a month later, others will bloom years later. What if you knew that every seed you planted would grow to fruition, but you didn't know exactly when? How many seeds would you plant? How many calls would you make? How many meetings would you hold? How many guests would you invite? It is so worth it to build big, and build fast. However, make no mistake, most prospects will not follow up with you. Diligent follow-up on your part is required.

My Advice to a New Associate

Your level of belief in yourself, the system we run, the company we represent, and the products we provide, can drastically affect your outcome and the speed with which you succeed. Many before you have already done the research. There is no need to reinvent the wheel. Go all in. You won't regret it.

Trust your leadership. They have your best interests at heart. This is not corporate America, where they only teach you enough so that you are not a threat to their job. We want you to succeed immediately. WFG is so serious about growing big and growing fast, with major nation-wide expansion, that our compensation plan is even designed for your immediate growth. Your leader is compensated on your production to ensure your success. The faster you grow and the better you get, the more WFG will compensate them. So you see, your leader has a vested interest in your success. Why wouldn't you listen to them? Why wouldn't you just be coachable and do exactly everything that they say? This can be the game changer for most new agents.

Duplicate, don't innovate. This is an arena where the more coachable you are, the faster your business can be successful. Those who come from other professions and try to reinvent our already successful model and show us how it's "supposed to be done," are usually very disappointed and set themselves up for possible failure. The old-fashioned financial services industry does not understand why we recruit those with little or no experience. It drives them bonkers. The reality is, I would rather not recruit someone from the industry who comes in with their bad habits and baggage, and tries to tell us how to change our system. I would prefer to recruit someone who is a blank canvas and train them the proper way to run our system. I firmly believe that we are soon to be the biggest and best financial services company in the world, and we will be ranked number one. I can virtually guarantee this will occur with the overwhelming majority of our agents and leaders coming from industries other than financial services. Eric Olson said, "When you become an EVC, you can make some changes. Until then, you need to follow the system exactly how it is written." Those are wise words from such a young man. Can an "old school" financial services person succeed in WFG? Absolutely! But, it will require extra doses of belief on their part, and mega doses of coachability.

Are you a producer, or are you an administrator? Very seldom in any sales arena is a person well versed at both. If you are a producer, you love to close, you love to sell, you love to recruit, and you love to write business. If this is you, get help! You will need someone to handle your paperwork and administration. To be successful, you will eventually need an assistant anyway. Believe me, the longer you wait, the more this is going to cost you in lost sales and persistency issues. With an assistant, you can go out and produce to the best of your ability because you have the proper support in the office to get it all processed.

Now, on the other hand, if you are administratively inclined, you need to go recruit some producers so you can override them all! Then, you can be in administrative heaven, processing their paperwork to get yourself paid. One of the secrets to my early and rapid success was in knowing which one I was when I walked in the door. I am a producer. So before I even walked in the door of my first office, two weeks after being licensed and only six weeks after getting coded, I hired an assistant. I knew that I could be the most productive producer in the world if someone else handled the paperwork, the licensing, and the lengthy interaction necessary to follow-up with the product providers. I would then have more time to go out and recruit, do one-on-ones, sit at client's kitchen tables, write policies, conduct meetings, do fast starts, and turn in business. Hiring an assistant also allowed me to always have someone in the office, answering phones, greeting agents and guests, getting things done, and being a presence so I could spend more time in the field. It was one of the best decisions that I have ever made.

My Advice to a Leader Who Is Stuck In a Rut

One of the major advantages in WFG is the accessibility to leadership. There is such an unselfish attitude that permeates our company. Seek out advice from those above you. Most are willing to share, give you a course correction, and assist you with getting back on track. Utilize the leadership resources available to you. They are plentiful. Be sure to always keep your attitude positive. Most obstacles on the road to success may appear as brick walls, but most are really just speed bumps that you can navigate over and around.

Get back out in the field. This is where the fun is. I love sitting at kitchen tables and putting families into a better place than I found them financially. I love changing lives.

Train new recruits and open up new markets. If this doesn't get you out of any rut, close the lid and have them start shoveling the dirt.

One of my favorite quotes is from Monte Holm. He said, "Quit majoring in the minors!" Too many leaders spend too much time at their desks, pushing pencils, shuffling papers, and doing non-productive things on the phone and the Internet. Give that administrative stuff to your assistant, and go get productive. It works every time. Action breeds activity. Lead by example. Go wide. Be a do-it-first leader. If you don't have your million dollar ring yet, why would you want to slow down? Get going and get it done!

Common Mistakes Associates Make

1) Being stuck in the corporate mindset. Congratulations! You have a code number. The good news is you now have your own business. The challenge is that you now have to run your own business. You can't think of this as a "9 to 5" job. First of all, you will need to be available when your clients are. If they are at work all day, you may have to put in some evenings and some weekends just to meet with them. Get used to it. Tell your family. Let them know you are building a better future for them. You may have to be out of balance for a little while in order to be in balance for the rest of your life. Believe me; it is well worth any and all temporary discomfort for the permanent gains that you can achieve. How out of balance do you need to be and for how long? Well, how much of your future would you like to own? Would it be worth it to work hard for five, 10, or maybe even 15 years if it means you can possibly be financially independent for the rest of your life? Most people are going to work hard for the next 15 to 20 years of their lives anyway, building another man's dream. Why not work just as hard and just as long to build your own dreams for your family? Most wealthy Americans did not achieve financial independence by working for someone else.

2) Giving up too soon. Too many agents quit right before they are about to make the breakthrough. Be patient. This is definitely not a get-rich-quick scheme. Some of us will take longer than others to figure out the rhythm that works best for us. If you are willing to stick it out, run the system properly, be coachable, and never miss a BPM or a big event, you will eventually figure it out. Many will end up doing extremely well for themselves and their families. As Eric Olson says, "Join, don't quit."

3) Waiting for people. You can't afford to wait for people to get it. You must keep recruiting. Just because you have a team, does not mean that you are set. Those who want success will pass by many people who think they have it all figured out. When you need three SMDs for your next promotion, you should have six potential SMDs lined up and competing with one another. Challenge them to win. The cream will rise to the top. When you are running an office with constant training, classes, BPMs, events, webinars, and conference calls, most people can find a way to succeed. I provide a nutrient-rich environment for growth. All agents have to do is show up, listen, learn, and implement.

Personal Challenges I Had to Overcome

I was blessed to be under the leadership of my nephew, Eric Olson. The downside was that Eric was in San Jose, and I was in San Diego. So my upline was over 500 miles away. Getting to Eric took either a two-hour plane ride or eight hours in my car. We talked daily by Internet, text messages, and even by fax machine. We used modern technology to bridge the gap. When your leadership is that good, how can you fail?

Again, I had to be completely coachable to my 27-year-old nephew. I remember the day he was born. I read books to him before he could read. But, I am also smart enough to know that he has already blazed the trail to success and he is at the top of this company. Who am I to question him? He is my upline leader. I am sure he made a mistake or two along the way. Why would I want to make those same mistakes? He has already got it all figured out. If I just follow his successful path and avoid his mistakes, I can accomplish success faster, right? My advice to you would be to follow the examples of success all around you. They are too numerous to count. They can get you there faster, if you are coachable and open to them. Our system is designed for you to grow faster than those who came before you.

Things I Would Do Differently If I Had To Start Over

I would have recruited more to our part-time opportunity. I was so sold out, my belief level was so high, and I was so convinced that this was an amazing business model that I must have asked the first hundred people that I interviewed to quit whatever they were doing to come aboard full time to help me build this financial services dynasty. Not too many were willing to give up everything to come aboard full time for a commission-only position. I now realize that most, if not all of them, would have been willing to try our business on a part-time basis, or even just become a referral agent. Currently, many of my most successful agents and brokers did come aboard part-time and then transitioned over to full-time when the cash flow was sufficient. It was an easy mistake to make. I did. Avoid it and you will grow faster.

My Vision for the Future of My Business

What attracted me to this company is that there are literally no limits to what you can accomplish, how big you can build your business, or how much money you can make. No limits! I like the sound of that. I can once again increase my income year over year for the rest of my life. I intend to fully take advantage of the opportunity to do so. After five short years, I have already opened four offices in San Diego, and we have opened ten offices in Florida. We have many more planned, and in the next five years, I will have offices in at least a dozen more states. Those seeds we are currently planting nationwide will be coming to harvest. There will be over 100 offices under my supervision in the next ten years. My team will be recruiting over a thousand agents and writing millions of points every single month.

Presently, with only five years under our belts, we are still at the beginning of our journey. There is so much more ahead for us. So far, WFG has changed the way we view life, money, and relationships. This business has strengthened our faith in God and brought our marriage closer together. Our lives have been reinvigorated. We have been allowed to dream big again, and can see that the fruits of our labors will affect our team and our family for generations to come.

Chapter 4
Johnny Velasquez

Seeing so many people become successful, whether it be in my peer group, on TV, or while watching my favorite sports teams win their championships, inspired me to do something bigger and better with my life. Going to school for nuclear medicine, I thought I had found my calling. When I took a part-time position in real estate, I was quickly entertained by the experience of chasing and accomplishing goals. Six months later, I outgrew any thoughts of going into the medical field and I took a chance on business. My parents were petrified of me going into business for myself, and they had every reason to be. I was 19 years of age with zero business experience and hardly any professionalism. Yet, 24 months later, I was established with my own real estate operation. And when it was good, it was good. But we all know what happened to real estate agents during the crash.

When I hear that "timing is everything" in our business, it takes me back to 2008 when my real estate business went from booming to bust. At a time when everything seemed to be unstable, a good friend of mine walked in with WFG leader Randy Sicairos and offered me an opportunity of a lifetime. It was a good thing Randy used other stories of real estate agents who transitioned into the WFG business. He put the business in my language and I was able to connect with it right away. It was from that point on that I knew the clear direction where I was heading. I no longer had uncertainty of what I was going to do or the income I was going to make.

I mostly loved the fact that I was going to be able to compete while accomplishing different promotion levels within the company. They say the best way to lift your identity is through competition, and competition drives performance. I liked the little wins that started to happen for me in the beginning stages of my WFG business. I enjoyed getting licensed, earning my first promotion, protecting my family's investments and lives, closing my first sale, and recruiting my first business partner. There were many little accomplishments that led to me planting my flag in this business. I am so thankful for this opportunity and will never take lightly the opportunity to help people secure their dreams.

The Keys to My Personal Success

I have a constant drive to improve as an individual - every single day in every single aspect of my life. I continuously strive to better myself in my relationships, fitness, faith, leadership abilities, and personal and spiritual growth. When I wake up in the morning, I look myself in the mirror and think of what I did the day before that I could have done better, and what I did that was great. I focus on areas needing improvement, and I make a commitment to be the best version of myself.

It is also important to be your, and your spouse's, biggest fan. Who else is going to wake you up in the morning and tell you that you are the best and that you can have anything you desire in life? Kaitlyn and I know that anything we talk about we can, and will, have.

No matter what is going on in your life, focus on the greatness around you. Anytime I am having a down moment, I take a few minutes to think of all the things I am grateful for. I am fully aware that the more you are grateful for, the more greatness you will have in your life. What you focus on is what you get, so it is very important to constantly strive to become the best version of yourself.

My Advice to a New Associate

If I could go back to the beginning, I would have leveraged my entire market with my trainer. Everyone knew me as the real estate guy, not the financial services professional. When I came into this business, I was so excited to share my new services with my real estate clients that I went to almost every single one of them on my own. The problem was that I had no leverage and no credibility as a financial professional. The week prior, I was selling real estate. The same goes for any new individual coming into this business. The majority of agents coming into WFG don't have prior industry experience. Of course that raises a red flag with your warm market.

For example, if a med school student was conducting free physicals and x-rays and discovered a problem that needed surgery, the patient would not want the student to conduct that surgery alone. They would invest in skilled care offered by an experienced surgeon. In this business, about 99% of the time, when an agent approaches their warm market with no leverage and no form of credibility, the same types of thoughts occur within the minds of prospective clients. They wonder, "Wasn't he working at Apple last week?" "I bought my home from him, I wasn't aware he was also a financial professional." "Is this someone I would trust with my entire life savings?" The questions are natural. Yet, because of our proven system, any individual with any background or level of experience can succeed in our business. The number one secret to that success, in my opinion, would be getting in front of every single person you know, right away, with an experienced trainer.

My Advice to a Leader Who Is Stuck In a Rut

Any leader who is stuck in a rut should take a look back at every single thing they have accomplished and recognize the amount of time it took to achieve those accomplishments. Because we are in such a fast-paced business, it can be very easy to get down on yourself for not being where you believe you should be in your business. Try not to get overwhelmed with stress about a promotion goal, a ring, or other areas of improvement. The best thing about our business is that every single day is a brand new opportunity to make a run at your goals and dreams. Our business is very forgiving. If you had a bad day, that does not mean you have to have a bad week. And if you have a bad week, you do not have to have a bad month.

Any leader who is stuck in a rut should also take some time to reflect on why they are in this business. Rewrite your goals and visualize the life you are on the way to having because of this business. It is so important to take a step back and reflect on greatness.

It is also important for leaders to get back to what gives them mental strength. Whether strength comes from family, faith, fitness, friends, healthy eating, or another source of happiness, leaders should take time to enjoy the things that help pump them up. This kind of focus will help you to reinvent yourself and give you a jumpstart to overcome any fears or slumps you may have. Once you've come out of the rut, you have to start sharing your experience with others. It's the best kind of experience you can go through to build your character and be able to help others overcome their struggles or adversities.

Common Mistakes Associates Make

New associates should not expect to achieve full-time results by putting in a fraction of the work effort. Sometimes, new associates play it safe. In this case, playing safe just means a lack of commitment, lack of intensity, and lack of determination. This business takes 100% effort, 100% focus, and the will to follow through in order to become successful. Once you take a chance, you might as well go all in!

I remember when I first started. I would have done a lot better and achieved success much earlier if I had gone all in from the very beginning. "No risk, no reward" is very true. Sometimes, you have to sacrifice things that are important to you, like your job, hobbies, friends, and even some of your family time. Making sacrifices is necessary in order to achieve the success that you deserve.

Many of us are overdue for success and feel that success should already be ours. If you've overcome a lot of adversity, you know you deserve it. When the WFG opportunity comes to answer your calling, your life will never be the same.

Personal Challenges I Had to Overcome

In my previous position, I only had to manage myself. When I came into this business, I had to overcome the challenge of not being a recruiter. In WFG, being a great leader comes with being good at organization, management, training, inspiring, and lifting others. Initially, I was not ready to take on that kind of responsibility. I also felt like I had to have a whole bunch of success before I could recruit others to follow me as a leader. I was 100% wrong about that.

I used to tell myself that it is hard to recruit. When I did get a recruit, they would end up quitting. Then, a meeting with Greg Kapp changed my whole business around. He was speaking at one of our events on the 48th Floor of the Transamerica building and he said that the biggest producers who focus on transitioning into recruiting usually become the biggest builders. As soon as he said that, I wondered if that could be me. He then explained that if you can close a sale, you can close a recruit.

After that, I made my first run at hiring 10 directs in 45 days as a Marketing Director. I applied the same process in a sales transaction, but used the benefits of the business and how your life could change for the better. Just 18 months later, we hit Executive Marketing Director and never looked back.

My mentality shifted during our EMD run, and I started to affirm that I am a world-class builder. Once I started putting it out there, it was all attracted to me. Your affirmations will always come back to you if you have the courage to declare them publicly.

Things I Would Do Differently If I Had To Start Over

If I could start my WFG business all of again, I would have definitely focused on direct recruiting as my main objective. I would have introduced 50 directs into the business. I believe that 50 directs will allow you to get all the necessary skills you need in order to be a leader and run a successful business.

I also would have learned a lot more quickly how to fill out client applications, input AMAs, and complete illustrations. Going through 50 different experiences with direct recruits would have definitely sped up my learning process.

The funny thing about our business is that, even while stumbling through the learning process, you are still going to have some major successes for both yourself and your teammates. The business is really that good.

Getting 50 directs would also put you in a position to hit your SMD promotion. Getting 50 recruits in the next six months is one of my goals. If I could go back and restart from the very beginning, the magic number would definitely be 50.

My Vision for the Future of My Business

Our future is so bright! We all are going to be mega wealthy and fulfilled with happiness beyond belief. I see myself becoming a multi-million dollar earner with plenty of million dollar earners on our team. I envision a team of 3,000 licensed dreamers helping secure families futures. I will have an office in every single state in the U.S. I will have homes in Miami, New York, Los Angeles, San Francisco, San Diego, Cabo San Lucas, and Hawaii. My team and I will build plenty of leadership retreat getaway houses so we can bring our agency to enjoy great experiences. I see our team filling up a sports arena in the next couple of years because there won't be a room big enough to fit all of us.

Becoming a chairman of the company is definitely in our future, with lots of successful business partners leading a tremendous amount of EVCs, CEOs, EMDs, and SMDs. Our business is barely getting good, and we are only getting started. Changing people's lives for the better and helping them realize their dreams is who we are, not what we do. I see our team winning and staying number one forever. Team Legacy, Team Pinnacle, Team Infinity, and Team Fame are going non-stop, straight to the top!

CHAPTER 4
JOHNNY VELASQUEZ

Chapter 5

Kaitlyn Groshong

I always knew I wanted to be successful, have freedom of time, and attain financial independence. I never would have imagined my path beginning the way it did. I grew up with two younger brothers and hard-working parents. In my household, we never talked about money, I wasn't allowed to ask for it, it rarely came up in discussion, and, if it did, it was likely to not be positive. My parents always told me I could be anything I wanted - the sky is the limit. Along with that, if I wanted to be successful, I had to go to school, get good grades, go to college, and get a safe and secure job with benefits. I was torn. I saw them dream big, but time and time again they had to limit their dreams based on the income they were making. I held onto the aspect of dreaming and declared for myself I would make all my dreams happen.

My dream was to become a commercial pilot. I wanted to travel the world, make great income, and have freedom. It was exciting when I got accepted to flight school. At the same time, a harsh reality set in when I identified we did not have the savings for it. So, I began working to pay my way through community college. I found myself at a salon and loved it. I built great relationships with the owners, acquired sales experience, and learned how to run a business. I became number one in sales and earned a promotion to manager, all while going to college. They even had plans to grow and expand locations. I had a stable income, so I moved into my own apartment, bought a car, and got a credit card. Everything was going just right.

Shortly after the start to my young adult life, the owners of the salon sat me down and notified me that, due to the 2008 economy meltdown, things needed to change. They couldn't afford to pay me what they said they would, so I was obligated to find part-time work. I picked up a serving job at a restaurant. I quickly identified that wasn't enough, so I got a third job at another restaurant.

One thing I developed was tremendous work ethic. I was putting in 16 hour days, seven days a week, totaling 100-hour work weeks. School was on hold and working to pay my bills was a priority. Then one day, exhausted from being over worked and under paid, I started to reflect. What am I doing here? Why am I working so hard if I'm not thriving financially? I was still living week-to-week and paycheck-to-paycheck. I started to dream that something better would come my way. It's amazing how what you think about, you bring about.

One night at the restaurant, an old friend popped in. I always knew him as successful. He made a great income, traveled, and had a lifestyle I wanted. He shared with me that he had just qualified into business with a new company and he asked me how things were. I informed him of my situation. He told me with my work ethic applied in this business I could really build something for myself. When I came into his office and was introduced to the company, I was blown away by the examples of success. I knew if anyone else could make a multiple six figure income, even into seven figures, so could I. But I was also very curious. How do you make such great income? Where I come from, it was not very common. Yet, here is a company where just about everyone I met was making six figures or more.

When I was exposed to what we do as a company, I saw the vision. They said we teach people how to protect their money and build wealth. Immediately, I thought of my grandparents. They all retired, and they all went back to work. Either they didn't plan properly, lost money in the market, or didn't save enough. I was intrigued.

And then they shared with me the power of passing down a legacy rather than liabilities. What did that mean? When the picture was painted, my heart sank. I thought of my best friend who was 25 and the sole bread winner of his household. He bought his mom a home and was paying the mortgage. He was also paying his older sister's college tutition. Then he unexpectedly he passed away. Not only the emotional devastation that came along with his passing, but the financial devastation, became even more painful when I realized there are solutions in place to protect families. And here is a company devoted to the education of all people, regardless of background or experience. The crusade was on my heart. I made it a personal mission to reach out to everyone I knew. I went full time in business in my third month, and never looked back. I didn't even put in a two-week notice at my three jobs, because I knew I would never have a job again. My journey as an entrepreneur and business leader had begun.

I am forever grateful that this business opportunity was introduced to me. The growth and success it has provided are just the start of what is to come. I knew this was the company that would lead me down the path to fulfill my dreams - my dreams to be successful, my dreams to control my time, my dreams to become financial free! My goal of becoming a commercial pilot has now translated to owning a fleet of jets where private pilots work for me.

I am blessed to be a part of a business that has broadened my horizon to see the power of owning a business rather than working for another man's company. This is the vehicle to get me to where I want to go. I am appreciative for my mentors and my team. We are 100% a teamwork environment. I love seeing people win big in their lives. I find joy in having associations that are about personal growth and development and stretching limits. Together, we are on a journey to become the best we can be, help others get to where they want to go, and we, too, will get to where we want to go.

The Keys to My Personal Success

The keys to my personal success are, first and foremost, my positive mindset. In every situation, there is a positive and a negative. What you choose to focus on is what will magnify in your life. I have always taken the positive route. We determine our future by the thoughts we think, so it's important to stay positive. What good does it do to think negative? I consider negative thinking as self-destructive. I choose to be my own biggest fan. I have faith and belief in myself and I know I am in control of my destiny. Things aren't always perfect. Success is never easy. Then again, nothing worth having comes easy.

I am also a very quick learner, and, more importantly, a quick implementer. When I learn something, either in a

CHAPTER 5
KAITLYN GROSHONG

mentorship training session or in a book, I want to implement it right away. I can't wait to try it! I learn best by doing. I'm not afraid to step outside of my comfort zone. I know the more I stay uncomfortable, the closer I am to where I want to be and who I want to become.

There's a saying I firmly believe, "Comfortable people live uncomfortable lives, and uncomfortable people live comfortable lives." Everything we want in life is right outside of our comfort zone. I am committed to staying uncomfortable!

My Advice to a New Associate

For a new associate, I would strongly recommend having full faith and trust in your leadership. They have a vested interest in your success. In our business, you cannot get to where you want to go without getting others to where they want to go. So, naturally, your leadership wants to help you succeed. They will only ever tell you something to help you and your business grow. My leadership has become my biggest push to get better. They have also become some of my greatest friends. They say a friend loves you enough to allow you to remain the same, a mentor loves you enough to push you to become better.

My Advice to a Leader Who Is Stuck In a Rut

It is very important to have your reasons why you are in business in front of you at all times. Always remember why you came into business in the first place. Who are you fighting for? What in your life deserves to be improved? What does your dream life look like? Your reasons have to be so big you couldn't imagine quitting on them. Maybe it's a loved one, an impact you plan to make on the community, or the lifestyle you want to live. I have heard that the richest lands in the world are cemeteries, because so many people die with the riches of their dreams left inside of them. You are in the right place, at the right time, with all the power to make your dreams reality. Unlock what is inside of you. It will be 100 times better than you can even imagine.

In addition to your reasons, you must have your goals and business plan. Dreams can only become reality when they are written down and said out loud. Chant them to the world. Tell people what you plan to do. You will attract all you need to make it possible. I look forward to reading my personal affirmations, goals, and business plan out loud twice a day. I feel unstoppable after I say them.

Knowing where you're going is energizing and motivating. Get focused on your reasons why and write your action plan to get there. Chances are, you'll create momentum and feel great about where you're going. Momentum is magic.

Common Mistakes Associates Make

One of the most detrimental mistakes I see associates make is they get caught up in where they are. They feel they don't have enough success or experience to attract a team. They get worried people will ask how much money they have made or accolades they have earned and this keeps them from moving forward. Here's a secret: The least important part about us is our past. It's in the past. And where you are right now, in this moment, is now in the past. So guess what is the most important part about growing into who you want to be and building the big and successful business you want to have? It's where you are going! Have vision and talk about where you're going. The amount of clients you will service this year, the promotion you are on your way to earning, the cash flow that you will make, the locations you will expand your business into, and the lifestyle upgrades you will be making for your family's future. It's not the success you've attained, it's all about where you're headed! Some may think it is an exaggeration, but it's truly an affirmation. When you tell the story of how you want things to be, eventually it will be.

Personal Challenges I Had to Overcome

The wonderful thing about entrepreneurship is there are no barriers or prerequisites to attaining success in business. Starting my journey as a young entrepreneur I did face some challenges regarding my age and my network. I started in business at age 21. Naturally I did not want to reach out to my friends and peers as most 21 year olds are not concerned with building a business and striving towards financial independence. My experience was that most of them are deciding what they want to do in life, still in college and looking forward to the next social gathering with friends. I knew early on if I was going to build a serious business I needed to work with serious people. I had to focus on growing myself personally, reaching into mature market places with people that would find value in my businesses services. I was once given a piece of business advice that changed my career, "When you talk to people you're afraid to talk to, your business will get the results you desire." Why are we afraid to talk to some people? Because they bring value! When I took this advice and implemented it, the results started to come. Also when I stopped looking at my age as a problem, it stopped being a problem. When people asked me my age, I would ask back if they wanted to know my age or if they wanted to know how much I could help them. Always play on the offense and know you have value to bring to the table.

Things I Would Do Differently If I Had To Start Over

I am so grateful for what we have built and how our legacy is just beginning. I am in awe of how many lives have already been impacted and how many more lives will continue to be blessed. Knowing how our decisions today impact so many people's tomorrows, I would have committed to reaching out to more people sooner.

I have learned that people need us more than we need them. Doesn't everyone deserve a golden ticket to their dreams? In our business, when we talk to people, we are offering that ticket. Why not give the gift of unlimited golden tickets?

I would also stress the importance of belief. Whether you think you can, or think you can't, either way you're right! I've learned that thinking, speaking, and expecting big results puts you closer to getting those results. If you think a goal is six months away, it will be. If you think it is three months away, it will be. So why not shorten timelines? Also, when you set a goal and work towards it, everything you need to accomplish it will come. So never let doubt set in. You don't have to believe it all yet, but just don't doubt it. Think big, believe big, and take big action!

My Vision for the Future of My Business

Every day, I take time to envision where I am going. I am filled with gratitude to know that my dreams are limitless and I have a legitimate opportunity to make those dreams a reality. One of my biggest blessings was meeting my fiancé, Johnny, in this business. We are an incredible team, best friends, and soulmates. We will celebrate our dream wedding on August 15, 2015, and we couldn't be more excited for this new chapter. Together, we are building our legacy for generations to come. We know we will hit the highest level of our company and becomes multimillionaires, and mentor others on how to do the same. The dream homes, luxury cars, fleet of private jets, finest dining, and exotic travel destinations are just some of the experiences we've had the pleasure of enjoying and know so much more is to come. More importantly, we know our example of a world class partnership, strong and happy marriage, incredible future parents, and true success, while being humble people, will inspire some of the greatest business leaders our country will ever see.

We can see the thousands of agents we are leading in our business achieving their dreams and goals. We envision ourselves traveling to our hundreds of offices throughout to United States and mentoring wonderful entrepreneurs on how to win big in business and in life. We can read the headlines in *Forbes* magazine that our great team will strive to accomplish. We can feel the charities that will impact the world because of our contribution. We can visualize our $500,000,000 net worth in the next 15 years. And, above all, we can close our eyes and look into the future and capture that day when we meet the best version of ourselves - fulfilled in who we are, knowing that we are our very best, and yet, having even more room to grow and improve.

We work hard today because we want to be an incredible example in what it takes to win big in marriage, in family, in business, and in life. We love that we have found the place where the fight for our dreams will become our reality, and our path will be the start for so many others to do the same.

CHAPTER 5
KAITLYN GROSHONG

Chapter 6
Michael Coleman

I was born on a little island in the middle of the Pacific Ocean called Guam. If you were to draw a line from Australia to Japan, and then draw another line from Hawaii to the Philippines, those lines would cross at Guam.

Guam was made famous for three things. First, Guam has been a key strategic point for the U.S. military. Second, Guam had an infestation of brown tree snakes that ate up all the birds. Because there are no birds, the island is overrun with spiders. Third, in the 70s and 80s, Guam was home to the largest McDonalds in the world.

My folks realized that there were really only three career paths on the island. The first would be working for the military. The second would be working for the city picking snakes and spiders out of trees. And, of course, the third would be working for McDonalds.

My dad decided that we needed to go someplace with more opportunities. So, he and my mom relocated the family to Seattle, which is where I grew up. My mom worked at Mitsubishi International. My dad worked at Seattle City Light and then drove a bus for the Seattle Metro. I often went to work with my parents. I would help my mom with filing or cleaning, or I'd ride along with my dad on his bus routes.

On nights and weekends, they volunteered at church. My dad did accounting and my mom watched the kids. I learned an incredible work ethic just by watching my parents run 12 to16 hour days and not think anything about it! And the fact that they volunteered on their off hours gave me an early sense of charity and giving to others. I realized that a charitable heart and giving to others is more fun and more remunerative than any purely monetary or personal gain motivations.

In the mid-80s, when I was about 12, my mom and dad got jobs at a consulting firm and we relocated to a suburb of Los Angeles called Glendale, California. My parents worked hard to put my sister and me into a private school, but there were times when I'd have an occasional unscheduled "vacation" month due to no tuition. But when you're in your early years, and you come from a loving family, you don't really put any value on money. I just didn't truly understand how hard my parents were working.

While I wasn't from money, a lot of my friends growing up came from a lot of money, and that was always difficult for me to figure out. Then I had a very strong lesson about money when I was about 14 years old. My friends decided that they wanted to start a rock band. I was assigned to the drums as my instrument, but I had no idea how to play the drums. Although I had an excellent sense of rhythm and mimicry, my ability to keep time was terrible and I was transferred to guitar duty. I didn't know how to play guitar either. So, I went to my dad and told him that he needed to pay for guitar lessons. He laughed and said that he would teach me. This was like when your dad would say he wanted to cut your hair. I thought that would be the un-coolest thing ever. So I said I wanted to take lessons from a prominent local music school and the lessons were $50 an hour. My dad smiled and handed me a business card of a chiropractor friend of the family. When I asked what it was, he said, "Call up Dr. Hales. He needs a receptionist."

So, begrudgingly, I started working as a receptionist at a chiropractic office to make enough money to pay for music lessons. Looking back, I now fully appreciate the sense of work ethic, discipline, self-reliance, and independence that my folks taught me, even though I didn't fully understand it or appreciate it at the time.

I graduated from high school in 1991 at the age of 17. My best friend, Chris, and I had plans to go to music school. Since I was 15, I had held an after-school job at a local software company, working in the mailroom and stuffing information packets for customers. After I graduated, I applied there for a full-time position so I could save up to go to music school. I worked there for two years and had saved up enough money – or so I'd thought. Chris and I had each saved up about $10,000!

In the summer of 1993, we jumped in the car and went to Boston. I wanted to study jazz guitar and music production. We enrolled in the summer program and intended to stay for the fall sessions. Then we got clever and decided to start asking around what the students nearing completion got out of the program for which we were about to sign up.

The five answers we got were nearly unanimous from the seniors that we met. They said that they 1) got a great education in music, 2) learned to network in the industry, 3) learned to book and play live gigs, 4) got access to world-class recording facilities, and 5) amassed a six-figure student debt.

That last one was a clincher. We talked about it and figured that would be a crippling amount of debt. So, we wrote down all of our questions, showed up early to class, stayed late, met with our teachers, and got all of our questions answered. They thought we were just really passionate students. In reality, we were just on a budget and needed to compress timeframes.

After the first round of questions got answered, we wrote down another set of questions based on those earlier answers and got those questions answered too. Our goal was not to learn everything, but to learn where the information was and how to draw our own conclusions. We wanted to learn how to learn in our industry. This would make us independent and self-reliant.

After six months in Boston, we were $10,000 poorer. But, we also had answers to all of our questions. So, we moved back to Los Angeles to start playing.

On nights and weekends, we played and wrote. By day, Chris and I went back to the software company to make money to fund our music habit. I got hired back to work in the IT department, and he got hired back as a software engineer/programmer.

During this time, Chris got diagnosed with a very rare form of cancer called chondrosarcoma. I spent every day for about a year and a half in chemo therapy with him. It was a debilitating form of cancer, which meant that I had to drive everywhere. Unfortunately, there was nothing the doctors could do and about a month before his 20th birthday, he passed away. He was positive all the way up to his last breath and his strength in the face of adversity has always been an inspiration to me. That inspiration has served as one of my whys to excel at this business. I kept fighting the good fight.

But every adversity holds within it a seed of a greater benefit. After Chris passed away, his parents were blessed with twins two years later. I was given the unofficial title of "God brother," which meant that I got all the fun stuff like baseball games and fun trips without the financial responsibility if anything happened.

In 1994, I wound up getting introduced to a service called AOL by a friend in the graphic design industry. He said that the Internet was coming and that it would be the wave of the future. I had another friend that, a year earlier, told me about this Internet too, so there was a little bit of a buzz. I asked my boss, the chief technology officer at the software company, if she had ever heard of the Internet. Just based on my curiosity alone, she promoted me to webmaster on the spot.

For a year, I worked in IT and was the webmaster for the corporate website. The marketing and sales team wanted me to transfer to marketing so they could have control of the content. The IT department wanted me to stay in their department so they could have control. The office politics were one of the reasons I wanted out of corporate America.

In the end, the marketing team won and I got transferred to their division and was given a quarter million dollar a month advertising budget for online design projects and media buying.

Every day was like Christmas, because the advertisers wanted my marketing dollars! I had gift baskets, concert tickets, sporting event tickets, and more. Gifts arrived almost daily on my desk. This was the heyday of the technology industry.

But by 1998, I needed a change. As the twins were turning two, Chris's parents asked me to come back to New Hampshire and spend some time to get to know them. I decided to quit my job and just go for a month. That that month turned into two years of living and working on their retired apple orchard in central New Hampshire. I had money saved and I retired and was happy.

Two years later, I got a job offer to work at a wireless Internet technology company in Florida. I did not want to go, but they gave me a decent salary and huge stock bonus. That was the end of the year 2000 and, unbeknownst to me, we were headed for some very bumpy roads ahead.

I was given the job of director of research and development for new technologies. My job was to test our network and implement new products into our product line. I was told that we had tremendous financial backers and that our company tracked their stock in lockstep. One company that was helping with distribution was MCI WorldCom. The other company helping us with infrastructure buildout was Enron. In fact, Enron was supposed to cut us a check for a capital infusion for millions of dollars. That obviously never happened.

Because I had no financial advisors, I invested my own money in our company stock, putting all my eggs in the proverbial one basket. When Enron and MCI WorldCom headed for imminent bankruptcy, and with the events of 9/11 in 2001, we knew our days were numbered and I lost my job.

Shortly thereafter, I got another offer to work at the advertising and graphic design company that I had earlier outsourced projects to as a webmaster and media buyer. I happily relocated to Los Angeles at the end of 2001.

At that firm, I was offered the position of senior vice president of operations in charge of accounting, payroll, human resources, sales, project management, and quality control. In a nutshell, I ran the whole company. After a couple years, I went from 40 hours a week to more than 100 hours a week in many cases. Unfortunately, my pay did not reflect my increase in hours.

At my peak of dissatisfaction at my job, I read two books that changed my life. The first was *Behind the Arches* by John F. Love and the second was *Moneyball* by Michael Lewis. I was inspired by the first book to look at the franchise model as a means to create financial independence. I was inspired by the second book to figure out how to build a team out of a hodge-podge of undervalued, but championship-level, talent that would go on to change the world. The seed had been planted and I decided to approach my boss about franchising our advertising and design agency.

I prepared a huge business plan outlining market trends, our numbers, how to package everything, and how the model would work. I even had a cash buyer for the first franchise. I only wanted a 5% ownership of the new franchises that we opened. He would get 10% and we would be multi-millionaires!

After a few weeks of constantly bothering him, he finally looked at the first few pages of my franchising proposal and called me into his office. He said that although it looked good, he did not want to pursue it as it would cost too much and would take me away from my core duties of running our current operations. I told him that I don't own any of our current operations, and he told me that it was a family-owned business. Since I wasn't family, I'd never own any part of it anyway. As a pittance, he gave me a bonus of about $1,000 for a project that we worked on for Warner Brothers, he gave me two personal days off, and he game me two tickets to a Dodgers game. Needless to say, I was enormously disappointed. What I didn't know was that those Dodgers tickets would change the course of my life.

I called up my friend, Michael "Woody" Wooderson and told him I had tickets. He had been involved with WFG for about a month, but he was scared to call me and talk to me about it. When I invited him to the game, he was overjoyed at the opportunity to have a captive audience in order to invite me to a BPM. He knew I couldn't run away.

On the way to the game, during the game, and on the way back from the game, Woody told me all about WFG. If you can imagine a seven-hour invitation, that's exactly what I got. But they say you can't say the wrong thing to the right person. I was at my peak of dissatisfaction at that moment.

He put my name on the guest list, I got a call from a lady named Jaime Villalovos confirming my attendance, and I came down on a Saturday morning. Wes Faria did the corporate overview and Dana Lagattuta did my follow-up interview. Jaime and Shawn's entire team was less than 30 associates attending that day's training and BPM.

And so were the humble beginnings that brought me to the path I am on now.

The Keys to My Personal Success

I show up, I work hard, I make progress on a daily basis, I help others win, I don't quit, and I don't miss meetings or big events. I make money at every level, recharge when necessary, and stay in control.

My Advice to a New Associate

Involve your spouse at every point. My wife, Heather, and I have known each other since we were basically teenagers. We worked at the same software company in the 1990s, but we were really just speaking acquaintances. Years later, I recruited a mutual friend who put her down on a Top 25. I did the appointment, and the rest is history.

In the early days, when we struggled to get the business off the ground, I had trouble delegating and asking her for help. I have found that sincerely asking her for help and honest feedback has really helped our business to grow. Heather has tremendous insight and an incredible perspective that I sometimes under-acknowledge, but have always appreciated. Recognize and appreciate your spouse in real life, not just in your head.

Model your business, attitudes, and actions after the master builders. When I was in the corporate overview, the first observation I made was that someone owned the office and I wanted to know who that was and how they got there. I wanted to know how to own an office. I remember meeting John Shin and he was an EMD. He filled the room with his presence and made me feel like a million bucks. I remember listing out all the qualities of a CEO and decided to just "act as if" I were the CEO.

I remember one day we had a huge training on a Saturday. I saw the training room door was open, so I poked my head in to see who was there. All the associates were gone and all the chairs were still out and the training room was a mess. But there was John Shin, stacking chairs and cleaning. I remember that John and I just quietly stacked chairs and cleaned until the room was spotless. I knew in that moment why he was a millionaire and I knew I would make it too. He was a business owner! I wanted that too.

Have a plan to get the top of the company. When I found out that there was a list of guidelines on what to do to get a promotion, I studied those guidelines with passion and intensity. Every day, I drew circles and visualized promoting out many SMDs and CEOs. My first business plan was to hit the top level in the company of SEVC and promote twelve SEVC legs.

I spent over 30 hours on my first business plan, studying the promotional guidelines and getting very clear on the amount of work it would take to get where I wanted to go. I kept those promotional guidelines with me everywhere I went and I had what I called a checklist mentality. I would just look at each requirement as a check box to be checked off. I never made it more complicated than that.

Simplify the plan down to something everyone can recite. I remember I wanted 10 offices. That is all our team talked about until we had 10 offices. To every teammate I'd spend time with, I talked about what it would mean to them to open an office. That was Phase 1 of my original plan. Now, Phase 2 is helping the leaders in those offices open 10 offices. We will have more than 100 offices opened in the next two years.

Be a leader and lead. I never waited for anyone to tell me what to do. My goal was, and is, to be the highest profit and lowest maintenance leader in Jaime and Shawn's organization.

My Advice to a Leader Who Is Stuck In a Rut

I think what causes people to be in a rut is the sudden overwhelm that can occur in the explosive nature of how our business grows. You can feel like you're dropping balls and letting people down. I read an essay in church called *How to Rise Above Your Troubles* that gave me an exercise that has always helped me remain calm and in control. Whenever I feel overwhelmed, I stop and write down all the things that I have my attention on – all of my troubles and difficulties – and list every task that is occupying even the smallest amount of mental real estate in my mind, including business, personal, work, family, and more. I just list everything that I would consider an overwhelming problem. Then I go back through the list and write down all the ways I can tackle each problem. Just by doing that, I start feeling better.

Common Mistakes Associates Make

Quitting. This is a mistake I see people make that is unfathomable to me. You get a license, learn a few words, come to some classes, and bring a few people. You get better at this over time and you become more efficient. You help people along the way and you get referrals. You follow up and keep helping others. Then an explosion happens and you win. Why would you give up?

Not Asking For Help. I've seen associates mistake a legitimate challenge for being negative. Then they spin around for weeks or months with no forward progress. Just ask for help.

Not Listening to the Team. Higher echelons of leadership in the military rely on information from the frontline in order to make informed decisions for the good of the entire time. I've observed, as people start to grow a team, they begin to ignore indications of stress in the team. This can cost relationships and be a serious step backward. Displaying humility and having trusted teammates within the organization will create a strong culture of mutual respect. I value the insight of everyone on the team and will often even ask the newest person for their point of view. I've always wanted to make this the best opportunity for the newest person on the team. The essence of good management is caring about what goes on.

Personal Challenges I Had to Overcome

I remember when I first got started in the business. I was at a BPM training and everyone was told to pull out a piece of paper and write down the biggest problem or adversity in their lives. We all folded the papers, put it in a hat and, once the hat was full, we all pulled someone else's problem/adversity out of the hat. Some people cried as they read the problem they pulled out. Others shook their heads. The trainer asked who wanted their own problem back and almost everyone raised their hand.

I've learned two of my favorite sayings in this company:

1)   All you can do is all you can do, but all you can do is enough.
2)   Everything works out right in the end. If it isn't right, it isn't the end.

Things I Would Do Differently If I Had To Start Over

I would do nothing different. If I did something different, then I wouldn't have what I have now. I don't live in the past, I look to the future. I love my life, I love my family, and I love the people I work with. I have had a plan from the very beginning, which I stick to and review daily. Because of this plan, my trajectory for accomplishment is awesome.

My Vision for the Future of My Business

Heather and I have an office in Glendale, California, with a total of twelve offices nationwide. I am absolutely outlet and new office crazy. An outlet in our business is defined as a licensed associate that can deliver products and our opportunity into the hands of consumers. I want to have 100 new offices creating 300 new licensed associates per month!

CHAPTER 6
MICHAEL COLEMAN

Chapter 7
Sofia Shah

When I was four years old, my parents decided to emigrate to the U.S. from Peru, seeking the American dream. The pursuit of the American dream, at times, felt more like a nightmare as we struggled to acclimate to an entirely different reality. As a child, I watched my parents labor and toil to build a foundation in this new country and, ultimately, a better future for me and my little sister. My mother was a caregiver and my father worked the night shift for the OC Register seven days a week.

Growing up in Huntington Beach, California, a primarily wealthy area, I felt the absence of money and resources every single day. However, it was out of this feeling of inferiority that I realized my greatest desire, which was to create an alternate reality, far from the one I experienced. I wanted a life filled with the loftiest prosperity. Of course, at the time, I had no idea how I was to become wealthy. Yet, I was as certain as the sky was blue that I would be.

I began playing the piano at a young age, in hopes of one day becoming wealthy as a famous musician. But when I graduated from high school, my intuition led me to pursue a math degree instead. I fell in love with pure mathematics and got accepted to a Ph.D. program at UCI after completing my bachelor's degree in three years from Concordia University. My path appeared paved and my future bright when I suddenly had a change of heart. The fact of the matter was that I was unwilling to spend eight more years in school without having the opportunity to work towards my true yearning of becoming wealthy. So, I did what every other ambitious individual did in the mid-2000s. You guessed it; I decided to try my hand at real estate.

Despite this short lived endeavor, for reasons I'm sure I don't need to explain, the experience was vital because I felt what it was like to be my own boss and control my own time. I instantly decided that having this freedom would be my ultimate pursuit. Once again, I had no idea how I would do this, especially in the midst of the financial tempest. Yet, I was still sure that I would.

During the time I was in real estate, I was recruited into WFG. I remember being super excited to have an additional business to supplement my real estate business. One of the first references that my mentor called was my pastor at the time. I was not sure how that conversation went, but my pastor called me right after they got off the phone and warned me that I had joined a pyramid scheme and the company I was with was a scam. My pastor had so much credibility that I took his word for it and quit the business immediately. It was at this time that my life took an unexpected detour and I ended up working as a sales rep for Verizon Wireless. It was at Verizon that I met my future husband as well as my business partner, Mo Shah.

While still working at Verizon, we decided to merge our lives as a married couple and start a family. Needless to say, this was no easy feat with the both of us working retail. I came to a point in my life where, on the outside, it seemed like I had it all - a new marriage, a five-bedroom house, nice cars, and more. But, I still lacked what was most essential to me - my freedom. My misery slowly started to eat away at me and I knew I could no longer remain in my current position.

One fateful day, as Mo and I were shopping at a local Target store, a somewhat timid, middle-aged woman approached us and asked if we were bilingual. It caught me off guard. I had no other choice but to engage in a conversation with her. I was shocked to learn that she was offering me a way out of my current situation. I jumped at the opportunity to check out an alternate career path.

I attended a WFG Business Presentation Meeting in August of 2009 and I instantly fell in love with everything the company had to offer. I loved the opportunity to be my own boss and own my own time, but I mainly loved the mission of helping families achieve financial independence.

Growing up the way I did, I knew what it was like to not have money. I figured if this is something that others can avoid and if I could be a part of the solution, my life would have meaning. Out of my desire to help others, I knew that I would do well financially. And if there was a way to do it on a grander scale, I knew I would become wealthy. After a few weeks of urging Mo to do the business with me, he finally conceded and we were off to the races.

The Keys to My Personal Success

The single most important key to my success is the continuous work I engage in to change my habits of thought. It is our job to be aware of our habits of thought or be ruled by our habits of thought. Most people seem to focus on the habits of behavior and then wonder why it is difficult to consistently perform at optimal levels. It is important to understand that our thought patterns drive our behaviors, which ultimately create the results that we get. It is imperative to spend time engaging in metacognition, which is to think about what we think about. If we have limiting thoughts or beliefs, it is our job to do everything and anything in our power to replace these with empowering thoughts and beliefs. Luckily, there are many ways to do this, such as talking to a mentor, reading a book, or being conscious of how we talk to ourselves. Unfortunately, we all come to this business with a set of beliefs that have been preprogrammed into our minds from the day we were born. If our goal is to become a multimillionaire, we have to adopt an entirely different set of beliefs about ourselves and the world around us.

My Advice to a New Associate

The best advice I can give a new associate is to understand the power of adversity. Our society has been programmed to look at adversity as something that should be avoided and feared at all costs. So when someone starts this business and they get rejected by a close friend or they fail their test, their mind instantly tells them that this is not for them because there is an opposing force hindering their success. Unfortunately, I learned this the hard way because, as I mentioned, I quit the moment my pastor told me WFG was a scam. I let the first sign of adversity deter me from all of the plans I had in starting my new financial services business. I did not learn this lesson until my second time around.

It is important to understand that without the opposing force of adversity, we could not grow and become as successful as we desire. It is in these times of temporary defeat that the seed of our strength is planted, which then allows us to reap the rewards of bigger and bigger challenges.

My Advice to a Leader Who Is Stuck In a Rut

If a leader is stuck in a rut, it is usually because they have lost sight of their goals. It is important for us to constantly be aware of where we are going, because this is what drives us. We need to have short-term goals, mid-term goals, and long-term goals. We need to look at these goals on a consistent basis and visualize ourselves achieving these goals. This process creates excitement because it is the pursuit for what we want out of life. Through the process of visualization, we will feel closer and closer to our goals. In feeling this way, our behavior quickly follows and the results come right after. Before we know it, we are out of the rut.

Common Mistakes Associates Make

I believe the most common mistake people make in this business is overcomplicating the system. It is hard for most people to understand that any system can be very simple. So, naturally, they want to add to it so it will make sense in their minds. I have learned to find beauty in simplicity and I believe this is something that most people will not understand right away. When they do, their business will explode.

Another very common mistake associates make is not having trust in the company or the products. This is very easy to do because most of us have never been exposed to a business like WFG so our reaction is to become skeptical and look for "the catch." The longer we stay in this state of mind, the longer it will take for us to get our business up and running.

People don't buy the product we are selling or the company we are with as much as they buy our belief in our product and/or company. The faster we can get sold out to what we are doing and what we have, the faster we will have results.

Personal Challenges I Had to Overcome

Over the past few years, I have had to overcome many personal challenges. First, being in the people business meant working with people and conversing with people. For me, this was very arduous because I was terribly shy and naturally introverted. I held a deep fear for everything that had to do with human interaction. Making phone calls, doing field trainings, prospecting, and public speaking were so far out of my comfort zone that many times I would take an hour prior to engaging in these activities just convincing myself that I could do it. But I would force myself to act in spite of my fears. Through repetition, these activities became a part of me and started to define me as a person. Then, out of my greatest weakness came my greatest strength.

Things I Would Do Differently If I Had To Start Over

If I were to start over, I would honestly not change a thing. This is by no means an attempt to say that we did everything in a perfect way, because it is quite the opposite. However, I would not do anything differently because it is this unique process which we have undergone over the course of the last few years that has attributed to our success. I respect that.

My Vision for the Future of My Business

I see WFG becoming the largest distribution channel on the planet for financial services. It is going to be hard for this not to become a reality because we have so many big thinkers that have created this reality and it is a force that can't be stopped. The foundation has been laid, and we are all reaping the benefits of the growing pains that many before us have had to endure.

Our organization will be at the forefront of this mega movement. Mo and I committed ourselves to a 10-year run to go all out, full effort. We started that run in 2010. We are currently focused on helping as many people as possible get to a leadership role as Senior Marketing Director. As a result of us helping many individuals reach their goals, we will become Executive Chairman before the end of our 10-year run.

Chapter 8
Mo Shah

I was born in Fountain Valley, California. I grew up as the oldest of three boys in a single-mother household. My mom, Maria Shah, is my hero. She raised three boys by herself while working multiple jobs. I saw how hard my mother worked to provide for us and I was inspired at an early age to not only retire my mom, but to be in position to give her the best lifestyle possible. I was relieved in 2010 when my mom found a great man, Ricardo Velazquez, with whom she would spend the rest of her life.

My mom and her family came to the U.S. from Afghanistan in the 1970s when the Soviet Union invaded the country. That sacrifice gave me another motivation to win for my family. At an early age, I made a decision that I needed to find a career to get rich. Playing sports was what I enjoyed the most, so I decided to work very hard to become a professional basketball player. I grew up playing basketball every day and my childhood idol was Michael Jordan.

After eighth grade, I went to the doctor's office for a physical. I was so eager to get the results of my projected height. I needed to be 6'6" in order to be the same height as Michael Jordan. The doctor offered good news and bad news. The good news was that I was healthy and my bones were growing strong. The bad news was that, if I was lucky, I would reach 6'2". I was devastated to say the least. I then researched my potential height and looked at football. I came to the conclusion that I was going to dedicate the next four years of my life to the football and try to make it in the NFL as a free safety on defense.

One of the best times of my life was playing football at Woodbridge High School in Irvine, California. I played all four years and made the varsity team in my sophomore year. Football taught me about the value of teamwork, mental toughness, overcoming obstacles, never getting too high or too low, and leadership.

Unfortunately, I didn't reach 6'2" and only received one letter at a Division III football school. I was a C+ average student in high school, and took summer school every year to get the tougher courses out of the way so I don't get too distracted with school work during football season. All of those extra summer courses allowed me to graduate early and get a head start at community college. I took 25 unites in my first full semester at Irvine Valley College, completed my associate's degree at age 18, and officially retired from school. I didn't see any more value in pursuing an education when I felt I hadn't gained any knowledge to be successful in the real world.

I started working at age 15 at the Marriott Hotel as a server to help support my family. I made it a point to save my money so I could get ahead in life. By the time I reached 18, I had about $20,000 saved up from my three years of working.

After I made the decision to stop attending college, I got hired at my first and only corporate job at Verizon Wireless. I was so excited to work hard and move up the corporate ladder. I started off in customer service and got promoted to retail sales. I was very competitive and wanted to be the best at my position. The biggest blessing I got from working at Verizon Wireless was meeting my beautiful wife, Sofia. We worked together at the Irvine Spectrum. We were a great one-two punch. Together, we made our location the number one in the region for about a year.

Sofia and I got married after a few months of dating, and we bought our first home in Riverside County, California. We had everything we needed when we got married. We had our jobs that provided a six-figure combined income. We had a beautiful, two-story, five-bedroom home. We had an exciting new marriage. And I was only 19 years old! I was in a position to live an amazing life starting in an early age. The only the problem was that we had no time to do anything with our lives, because the majority of our time was invested at our jobs.

One day, Sofia and I were shopping at a Target in Menifee, California, and we were approached by a lady and her son. She asked us if we were bilingual. Sofia is from Peru and speaks Spanish, so we said, "Yes." The lady told us that her company was expanding in the inland empire and they were looking for a bilingual power couple. We later found out that she cleaned homes for a living and was extremely shy, but the reason why she prospected us was because her five-year-old asked her, "Mom, wouldn't you like to have a successful young couple like them on your team?"

Sometimes in life, all you need is 20 seconds of insane courage and bravery. Sofia and I went to a corporate overview and we got on board immediately after the meeting. You can't say the wrong thing to the right person. It didn't matter what the opportunity was, because Sofia and I were ready to get into a business where we could work together and build an amazing legacy for our family.

Sofia and I committed to a 10-year run from 2010 to 2020 to make history for our family's legacy with World Financial Group. We hit our Senior Associate promotion by completing 10 and 10 in our first month in the business. Five months later, we hit our Senior Marketing Director promotion. We earned our $100,000 ring during our second year in the business. We then hit our CEO -promotion in our fifth year in the business. We retired my mom and Sofia's parents in 2014.

We just ran with the opportunity. We felt that no one could stop us. Our mission was to revolutionize the power couple in not only WFG, but in the entire financial services industry. In our five short years in WFG, we have been blessed to be featured inside Forbes magazine, and on the cover of Business & Finance magazine.

The Keys to My Personal Success

Sofia and I have huge goals and dreams. We are a power couple in business together. Most people laugh when they hear the story of what we want to achieve. We believe the only limitations are the ones we set on ourselves. I always say that two people can always do more than one person. It's a huge advantage to have a husband and wife work together in the business, but it's also important to be equally involved in all aspects of the business.

Our personal development has been huge. We have run our business by ourselves for our entire career, so we were forced to act like a CEO from day one. We had to go to all the big events and read the proper books to get ourselves in a position to lead a team. Our team is now privileged to have two leaders to help them win in this business, while we only had each other. And we would never want it any other way. We are blessed with the path that we were forced to go through. It's the main reason why we are succeeding.

My Advice to a New Associate

When you join our business, it's important that you make a 100% decision that you are going to make this business work for you. You need to write your own goals and your to-do list of what you need to accomplish throughout the duration of being in this business. Then you should talk it over with your family so they know how important it is to for you to get their support. After doing that, you must follow the system that your leader provides in order to go from a Training Associate to a Senior Marketing Director. You must get to that position quickly. That's where you can truly start to build this amazing business with the highest potential possible. I always tell my team that there are three main objectives in the business: hit SMD, build a big base shop, and promote frontline SMD leaders.

My Advice to a Leader Who Is Stuck In a Rut

If you are frustrated with your business or frustrated with your team and you feel like your business is not growing, then you need to find 10 to 12 new direct business partners in about a 60 to 90 day period. Not only will this explode your business, but it will change your life forever. Then you need to focus on double digit recruiting. I tell my team there are two rules to this business. Rule number 1 is hit double digit recruiting. Rule number two is never forget rule number 1.

Common Mistakes Associates Make

The biggest reason why 90% of SMDs never promote an SMD is because they don't work on their personal development as a leader. You need to master leadership and human nature. The biggest mistake I see people make is that they take things personally from their teammates during difficult situations and they let it turn into a clash. You need to treat your associates like your clients. You cannot get offended by people because it's just human nature.

There are three stages where people quit the most during WFG. The first stage is the first three weeks in the business. People are confused in the beginning because they have an employee background and they just joined a business opportunity. I tell my new associates to stay confused but stumble forward. After they have attended a few BPMs and completed the eight speed filters, then they built a habit and pass stage 1.

The second stage where people quit is during their first 90 days in the business. This is the toughest stage and where we lose the most people. This is the time that someone has to get licensed, complete field training, hit their promotions, understand the system, consistently trust their leaders, and be coachable, all while juggling their development process with their jobs and family. The most important part of this stage is to get someone licensed, field trained, promoted, and cash flowing $1,000 of income.

The third stage where people quit is during their first year in the business. I start this stage from the time someone gets their first paycheck in the business. Again, it's a new business. They need to hit SMD and get good at making income consistently. Nothing in life is easy the first year. But remember, you are dealing with human nature and people in our society tend to quit during adversity rather than digging deep and getting through it. From my experience, the majority of people end up making it in the business when they stick around after their first year, especially when they hit SMD.

Personal Challenges I Had to Overcome

Sofia and I had to sacrifice about 18 months of paying the price. We cut out sports, family gatherings, vacations, and spending money on things we wanted. For those 18 months, we worked harder than we ever had in our lives. We were doing 16 hours a day, seven days a week. We had to pay the price and build our base shop.

I stopped spending time with my close friends because our mindsets were not the same and I could not afford to be in their environment. I remember having appointments on Super Bowl Sunday, and coming home to sleep instead of watching the game because I was so tired from the grind. But it was so worth it. I would rather bust my butt for a shorter time in the right vehicle then remain stuck in the wrong opportunity for more than 30 years. Entrepreneurship is living a few years of your life like most people won't so that you can spend the rest of your life like most people can't.

I also had to check my ego and pride when it came to working with higher identity people. I had to adjust to working with people who had been successful before in other businesses. Our business exploded after we started to attract people that were better than us.

Things I Would Do Differently If I Had To Start Over

If I had to start over, I would immediately lower my overhead. When we started this business, we had an overhead of someone making $120,000 per year. Yet, when we went full time, we didn't lower our overhead and it hurt us financially.

I also would have gotten my securities licenses immediately. It gets much harder later on because you get busier in the business and it's difficult to find time to get them done, especially when your team is bigger.

My Vision for the Future of My Business

We made a 10-year commitment to build an amazing business. We are now past our halfway point. Our biggest focus is building independent outlets. We want to promote as many SMDs and CEOs as possible. My brother, Nick Shah, is in the business with me and he will become a CEO in 2015. My youngest brother, Noor Shah, is turning 18 in 2015 and I'm excited to get him going in the business as well. My mother raised three CEOs. That's an amazing accomplishment!

Sofia and I have our whole lives planned, all the way to our eulogies. We are looking forward to having children soon and using our experience in WFG to become amazing parents. It's an amazing blessing to plan and know where your life will be throughout each and every future decade.

Sofia and I will be celebrating our 10-year marriage anniversary in 2018, and we are looking forward to seeing how many people we have impacted just from our marriage in WFG. This business has been the vehicle to reach all of our goals and dreams. We are now focused on getting our leadership team in the Shah Dynasty to CEO so they can write their own stories in a book about their amazing lives and accomplishments.

Chapter 9
Rochelle Cherniawski

I grew up in western Michigan in what you might consider the average American family: mother, father, son, daughter, and dog. My dad worked for the same company for 28 years and my mother was a self-employed beautician. I was taught that you go to school, get a good job, and stay loyal to your employer.

During my junior year at Michigan State University, I met and fell in love with a fellow student who had a very different perspective. Michael Cherniawski didn't believe in the dream of chasing success in corporate America. On the contrary, Michael had every intention of being a self-made man.

You might imagine the struggles of a corporate-minded woman and an anti-corporate man. I found security in my full-time job at an advertising agency while Michael felt the stinging dissatisfaction of working for someone else. He tried a few side projects to satisfy his entrepreneurial spirit. Unfortunately, each one ended up taking his time and never bringing the promised return of money. Although I found each new opportunity to be endlessly frustrating, it was just the two of us and I really thought he would eventually appreciate the value of corporate employment.

When we moved to Florida, Michael was offered a position at Merrill Lynch and I joined a local marketing team. After a couple years of chasing millionaires, Michael decided to join a private venture. But, when I got pregnant, he got serious about doing whatever he needed to do to get us out of debt and prepare for the arrival of our son. That meant heading back to a corporate office by day and waiting tables by night. Ultimately, this is the experience that made me trust that Michael would never let me down.

While his first year got off to a rocky start at his office job, he hit the target of getting us out of debt and was able to drop the restaurant gig. And with his full attention focused on his new goal, he became the number one salesman in the global company in just his second year! I was so proud of him. As an added bonus, we got to go on the company trip to Maui.

This is the part of the story where my spousal support gets put to the test. It all started on that celebratory trip to Maui. We decided to break up the journey westward by stopping to visit with Michael's Uncle Chip and Aunt Linda in San Diego. Let me just tell you, I don't think we were even buckled into the car when Uncle Chip started praising Michael for all of his success. He was laying on the compliments so thick I had to roll down the windows to catch my breath! All joking aside, Uncle Chip was proud of his nephew and wanted to tell Michael about an opportunity that he discovered though his other nephew, Eric Olson.

I don't think Uncle Chip realized that we weren't interested in making any career changes. Oh wait. Let me rephrase that. I don't think I understood that Michael was practically drooling over the opportunity that Uncle Chip was presenting to us.

By the time we actually made it to Maui, it was clear that absence really does make the heart grow fonder, because Michael couldn't stop thinking about WFG.

His interest in WFG got kicked into overdrive when Eric Olson called him to compare success stories. It was hard to witness Michael being emotionally pulled away from his job. You can just imagine how I was feeling. Yet, I decided to show my support by suggesting that he try it out on a part-time basis.

That is when I learned that Michael doesn't understand the meaning of part-time. He literally worked all day at his full-time job and turned around to work the rest of the day, and into the night, on WFG. Eventually, I understood that he would need to commit 100% of his efforts to WFG in order to find success. On top of that, I didn't want to be the one to hold him back and beg him to stay in a job that meant he was living his life on someone else's terms. My only advice at that time was that he didn't burn any bridges on the way out, just in case he needed to go back.

The Keys to My Personal Success

In the corporate world, I found success through following the rules, working hard, and climbing my way up the ladder. As a supportive spouse in this business, my personal success is related to my mindset. First, I tend to look on the bright side of every situation. Second, I try to take a step back and consider the big picture. And when it comes to supporting my husband during trying times, I think about alternative scenarios. For example, when I get frustrated that he is working long hours, I think through the various careers that would cause a spouse to work long hours: truck driver, traveling salesman, doctor, restaurant manager, etc. If that doesn't seem to be changing my perspective, I think about what would happen if he started a new business and didn't put his heart and soul into his work. What if he slept in every day, came home for lunch, and debated on whether he wanted to go back to the office? I would tell that guy he was doing the wrong thing!

I like to think outside the box, I find humor in just about every situation, and I don't take things too seriously. These habits have helped me support my husband throughout some phases in our marriage that made me want to cash in on his life insurance policies. Catch my drift? Really though, I tend to be pretty laid back and I understand that what is a hot-button issue in the present moment is likely to be small potatoes within a matter of days, or even hours. I hate to waste energy on things I can't control, so I try to keep calm and carry on.

My Advice to a New Associate

Plan to get discouraged. Sorry. It's true. This business is tough. You have to be tenacious in your drive for success.

Be coachable. When your leader offers advice and direction, take action.

Don't feel like you need to know everything. Greg Kapp has a great saying about that. You should ask him sometime.

Toughen up. If you are sensitive, you are going to get your feelings hurt. If you have to walk away, do it. Then leave your feelings somewhere else and get back to the grind.

Recognize the great things that are in your near future and appreciate that your personal struggle will inspire others when you get to share your story from the big stage.

Learn to lead from the front. Be the success you want to see in the office.

My Advice to a Leader Who Is Stuck In a Rut

Get out of your comfort zone. There's a reason why it's called the comfort zone - it's comfortable. But, if you want to get out of that annoying rut, you have to be willing to grow out of it. Although growth can be uncomfortable, there's good news on the other side: you are about to be introduced to a version of yourself that you never even thought was possible.

Sometimes, more experienced agents start to overcomplicate things. They forget to keep it simple and follow the system. While that way of doing business might work for them, it doesn't work for recruiting because it's not duplicatable. Go back to the basics.

Common Mistakes Associates Make

One of the biggest mistakes that people make in this business is trying to do it their way. Don't get me wrong, one of the greatest benefits of this business is that you have the freedom to do things your way. However, perhaps the best benefit of this business is the proven system that is handed to you on a silver platter. Don't pass the plate, take it all and run with it!

Also, sensitivity can crush a business before it's even built. If you are too sensitive to handle a simple "no," talking to people is going to seem like a daunting task. Likewise, if you are too sensitive to handle advice from your leaders, growth and development in this business is going to be a constant uphill battle. If you are too sensitive to read this advice, I encourage you to go get a hug.

Negativity can also crush a business. I don't know anyone who enjoys working with negative people - as a business associate or a client. Negativity is like the invisible force that sucks all of the energy out of the room. I'm not saying you have to whistle your way into your office every morning, I'm simply suggesting a positive approach to daily interactions. That goes for social media as well.

I wish I didn't have to include this one, but trash talking can crumble your credibility and damage your associations. Just don't do it.

Finally, be strategic about what you share with your spouse. I almost can't believe this is one of my points, because I'm on the receiving end of this advice. Think about it though. Is your spouse going to be fired up about this business if you come home every day with messages of frustration and disappointment? Heck no! You have to share the good news with the man or lady in your life and get him or her excited about the future. When Mike was first getting started, he will be the first to admit that he was pretty terrible. Yet, he constantly told me good news about the development of our business. He forwarded me the text messages when he got paid. It took me a while to realize that he got two text messages each week, but he was only sending me a couple a month. He did that because he only wanted to share good news with me and get me excited about his progress. It's funny, but it's true. He knew what he was doing!

Personal Challenges I Had to Overcome

The biggest challenge I had to overcome in the beginning was the fear of change. I had to put on a happy face and tell my husband that I supported him cutting out his bread-winning salary and going to into the wild west of WFG. There was zero WFG presence in our market, his closest business contact was in Atlanta, and his direct upline was in California. Sure, Honey! Go ahead! You can do it! I believe in you!

Another challenge I had to overcome was my grave fear of public speaking. I'm the person who got nervous when it was my turn to give a simple status update in our weekly staff meeting. So, hand me a microphone and throw me up on stage in front of 2,000 people and my legs turn to crumbling ice and the words coming out of my mouth sound like a foreign language to my own ears. Not awesome.

Most recently, I had to get over the fear of leaving my job and joining my husband in this business. I worried about giving up my salary and benefits. I worried about finding my place in the office. I worried about living up to Michael's expectations. I worried about walking out of the bathroom with my skirt tucked into my tights. Seriously, I worried about every possible angle. But, in the end, I knew that I had to give up my worries and join my husband in this life-changing venture.

Another struggle has been showing non-stop support for a spouse who isn't home or available as much as I would like. That was even truer when I was working my own job. During that time, when everything was still new, I felt like I was constantly fielding questions about Michael's whereabouts. That's when I started to put my alternative thinking to use and realized that I was truly proud of him for his drive and commitment. I knew that he was sacrificing time with our family for the ultimate benefit of our family.

Now that I've started working with Michael and our lifestyle has become uncommonly common, I feel as though I've had less questions of concern and more words of support from my friends and family.

Things I Would Do Differently If I Had To Start Over

I wish I cared less about what other people think. I tried to buy something with other people's opinions the other day, but they didn't pay the bill. I've cared way too much about what other people think for my entire life. I don't know if I will every fully get over that, but I can tell you that I am actively trying.

I would also get better at recruiting. I'm still working on that. I understand the power of recruiting, and I know that we are always just one recruit away from an explosion, but I could definitely improve my recruiting chops.

My Vision for the Future of My Business

While my direct involvement in the business is still fresh, I am looking forward to being a more strategic partner in the overall development of our team. I know that we have only scratched the surface in regards to building Florida and I have a hard time wrapping my mind around the sheer magnitude of where we are going, or should I say growing?

At each big event I attend, I am blown away by the numbers that are presented regarding the future of our business. I am so thrilled that we took a chance when we realized we were in the right place at the right time. And I'm even more excited that we have a strong team who recognizes the great opportunity before us and we are all committed to growing together and celebrating our successes together.

In just two and a half years, we have connected with amazing leaders who are committed to building it big, and I know there are so many more people out there who are eager to find an opportunity that's even half as good as what we have before us. I can't wait for the day that Xtreme Team has a strong presence in every city across the great state of Florida… and beyond.

CHAPTER 9
ROCHELLE CHERNIAWSKI

Chapter 10
Michael Cherniawski

As the oldest of seven children, I grew up working for the things I wanted. When I asked for an allowance, my father bought me a lawn mower and told me to go out and make my allowance. He also told me that I was going to pay him back for the lawn mower! I quickly dominated the local market and had an army of neighbor kids working for my new business. The money was great and, naturally, I blew it all on frivolous things.

In addition to mowing lawns, I became a stellar filer and paper shredder for my father. He has been in the financial services industry for more than 45 years now, and I grew up seeing and understanding the value that this industry provides. Yet, I knew I wanted to carve my own path in life and do something different.

The pursuit of a college education led me to Michigan State University. To fund my education, and extracurricular activities, I put my childhood lawn mowing business on steroids and marketed myself as an estate management specialist in local neighborhoods with multi-million dollar homes. I met Rochelle in my final year at MSU and knew right away that I wanted her by my side for the rest of my life.

After college, I did what was expected – I got a real job. And, as I expected, I hated it. I liked the camaraderie of friendly competition with my co-workers, but I didn't like the feeling that I was getting short changed for my efforts. I constantly had my eyes open for other opportunities. I tried a few different things on the side, but didn't find the type of success I knew I was capable of achieving. In the meantime, I was driving Rochelle crazy.

When we moved to Florida in 2007, I took a shot at the financial services industry and joined a successful team at Merrill Lynch. The novelty of that position wore off pretty quickly as I realized I was going to be stuck behind a desk for the rest of my life without any ownership. Plus, we weren't allowed work with someone unless they had at least one million dollars.

When the stock market crashed in 2008, I determined that the old fashioned industry wasn't for me. At that time, I was unaware that a more modern approach to the industry even existed. I knew that if I wanted to be wealthy and do my own things on my own time, I would have to own my own business.

On my way out the door at Merrill Lynch, I ran into a younger guy from church who sold a company for hundreds of millions of dollars. My eyes were the size of dinner plates and I was drawn to an opportunity to partner with him on a start-up.

Unfortunately, the start-up didn't start up. I was at a high point and a low point in my life. We were pregnant with our first child, but we only had $300 in the bank. I knew I had to get serious about providing a strong foundation for my family. So, not only did I secure a position at a global technology consulting firm, I also got a job waiting tables. I set a goal to eliminate our debt and I got after it with fierce tenacity.

In the first year at the technology firm, with the understanding that I had unlimited income potential, I set a huge goal. I was actually laughed at and told my goal was impossible. To the amusement of my coworkers, I failed miserably. Did I care? Nope. I set an even higher goal the next year. And guess what? I actually hit it. And guess what? I was the number one salesman in the entire company that year. Boom! As a reward, the company flew me and my wife to Maui a day early for the all company qualifier trip. On the way to Maui, we stopped in California to visit my Uncle Chip and Aunt Linda. That's when I first learned about WFG.

I couldn't stop thinking about WFG the entire time we were in Hawaii. And I continued to think about WFG as my company handed me my reward for my remarkable accomplishment – a generic piece of glass.

When we returned to Florida, I got a call from my cousin, Eric Olson. He told me that he had heard about my success. Then he asked me how I was able to live on my income. We laugh about it now, but it really hit home. It made me rethink who was I comparing myself to regarding my personal success.

I got coded in April 2012 and went to the convention in Las Vegas that summer.

As I dipped my toes into the world of WFG, I learned that in order to move forward at my job I would have to displace my family and relocate across the country for a position that would have raised my quota to offset the increase in pay. WFG just kept making more and more sense. WFG gave me something to get excited about!

The beginning was not easy. My closest WFG business contact was in Atlanta, my direct upline was in California, my wife was nervous, and I was terrible. In that first year, I made just over $5,000 dollars part time. Even then, I sold the dream to my wife and went full time at the end of 2012.

The Keys to My Personal Success

My belief in this business and my vision for the future is what got me through the awkward start-up phase. I knew that if I was going to do this, I couldn't settle for mediocrity. I knew there was an opportunity to do something big and be truly significant. MY WHOLE LIFE (right Eric?) I just wanted to do something big. The opportunity fell into my lap during that fateful trip out to my Uncle Chip's house, and I wasn't going to let it pass me by.

I embraced this business as a chance to not only help a lot of people, but change the industry on a greater scale. I saw the limitless growth of this company and I wanted to be a game changer. I have always worked hard, but I can tell you from experience that it's much better to work hard to build your own business than someone else's.

With that, I committed to being coachable. I'll admit, at first I wanted to create my own system. But it didn't take me long to figure out that my way wasn't working. When I listened to my leaders and started following our proven system and teaching others to do the same, our business exploded.

Another key to my success is my competitive nature. I only compete against the best. I asked Eric about his records and what I had to do to beat them. I also looked at other success stories in the company and challenged myself to be the best. But, it's important to note that I always compete with respect for my leaders.

My personal success can also be attributed to investing my time and energy in people who are committed to greatness. Early on, I wasted too much effort trying to convince people and coach people who weren't giving anything back in return.

Now I focus on helping build and develop leaders who are hungry for growth.

A strong work ethic became one of my habits from an early age. As the oldest of seven children, I really didn't have a choice!

I have a giant vision and high expectations. I am committed to doing whatever it takes. If that means losing out on a couple hours of sleep, so be it. Some people say they will sleep when they are dead, I say I will sleep on the beach during my next vacation.

I am willing to get out of my comfort zone to reach and exceed my goals. In the beginning, every single step of the learning curve was awkward and uncomfortable. But, the more I pushed through, the better I became. And, now I'm using that awkward stage as a recruiting tool. I call people who I reached out to in the early stages of building my business and I say, "Hi, it's Michael. Listen, when I first started in this business, I was a little off my game. Now, two and a half years in, we are in a whole new ball park and I want to invite you to take a second look."

I also stay closely connected with my leaders and mentors. I'm accountable to them, I reach out for advice, and I follow their directions.

My Advice to a New Associate

This business is not a free ride down easy street. If you say you are going all in, then you need to back it up. I recommend frontloading all of your work in the beginning to build momentum.

You also need to build your belief. If you need a little help, simply borrow someone else's belief. You can find plenty of it at big events! In fact, make sure you attend a big event as soon as possible, even if that means you have to fly across the country.

Follow the system and don't complicate it. You've heard it before, so why are you fighting it? The system works! If you want to succeed, simply follow the proven steps to success. As Greg Kapp would say, "Simplify to multiply."

Be coachable. Your leader is incentivized to help you succeed quickly. It's a win-win. Being coachable is your secret weapon to building your business quickly.

Set specific goals and plan your time strategically to meet those goals. It's a shame to watch people waste time and, in turn, fail to see their business take off.

Get your significant other involved in the business. Invite your spouse to big events, introduce your partner to your team, and share your vision with your significant other.

Understand and respect the journey. I am not afraid to tell people that I was horrible when I first started. I think it offers hope for people to know that I started from scratch, made a lot of mistakes, and hit CEO in two and a half years.

The best way to build a solid foundation is to understand how the system works and then teach others how the system works. The faster you commit to that, the faster your business will grow. Again, this business is built on the basis that helping others get to where they want to go will, ultimately, will get you to where you want to go.

My Advice to a Leader Who Is Stuck In a Rut

Recruit. It used to drive me crazy when I called my Uncle Chip to discuss an issue and he would tell me to go out and get a recruit. But then I realized he was right. Just about every problem you will face in this business can be solved by recruiting. Not making enough money? Recruit! Having a bad day? Recruit! Team losing steam? Recruit! Having a disagreement with a team member? Recruit!

I also want leaders to consider what they communicate with their team. Please don't complain to your team. You are a leader. If you are having an issue, reach out to your leader or mentor. Then, go out and get a recruit!

Have you seen Men in Black? They use a little, flashy, blinking device called a neuralizer to erase memories. Sometimes, people who are struggling in their business just need to neuralize it and start fresh.

Go back to the basics. Get a new recruit and train them to run the system.

Another great tool for jump-starting your business is to participate and compete in Elite Circle. And challenge your team to do the same. Growth stimulates growth.

Finally, take a hard look at your business activity. Are you attending all big events? Are you getting your team to big events? How many calls are you making each day? How much time do you spend prospecting? How many appointments are you holding each week? What time do you get to the office? What time are you leaving the office? What is your daily schedule? Identify the areas that need improvement and get to work!

Common Mistakes Associates Make

1)   Stopping short. This business is built to move fast and many people put on the brakes from the get go and kill their momentum before it's even built.

2)   Reinventing the system. A lot of people try to rethink this business and do things their way. If everyone would just appreciate the value of the proven system in the beginning, this business would be growing even faster that it is today.

3)   Not working smart. I follow Jeff Levitan's example. He says, "I'm either in an appointment, or on the phone setting appointments. That's it. That's all that matters."

4)   Quitting. We've all heard stories from giant leaders in this business who lost their direct upline. Don't let that be you!

5)   Having a short-term mindset. Some people simply need more time to get really good. You have to think and act long-term in order to find true success.

It would be a grave mistake to ignore the benefit of being able to leverage the power of others who are successful in this business. I have learned so much from the great leaders in this company and I intend to continue using their success to my advantage.

A more obvious pitfall is stopping. The beauty of this business is that, if you build it correctly, you should be able to walk away for a period of time and your business will continue running and even growing. But, if you stop or take too much time off prematurely, you can reverse positive momentum and struggle to restart.

Personal Challenges I Had to Overcome

My greatest challenge was starting over from scratch, and convincing Rochelle that it was a good idea. But I am living proof that the system works because, for the most part, I had to just follow specific directions and do it.

Another challenge was training myself to become mentally tough. As I have discovered through this business, I am more emotional than I thought and I tend to take things very personally. Being mentally tough is a discipline. As Eric Olson says, "Getting rich isn't for sissies!"

Things I Would Do Differently If I Had To Start Over

I would have believed faster and done everything faster. This whole time, quitting was never an option. I have not done anything on the side, but I started too slow by staying in my full-time gig in the beginning. This is everything to me and my family and I only wish I would have hit it harder from day one.

I wouldn't waste a second trying to do things my way. I would implement to the speed of instruction and follow the system point by point. And I would have pushed faster through the early and awkward phase. Hesitancy and discomfort definitely blocked my productivity in the beginning.

My Vision for the Future of My Business

Xtreme Team Florida hit CEO at a record pace, and I intended to have our team continue to set records as we explode throughout the state of Florida. I envision that the future of the sunshine state will include a McDonalds, Starbucks, and WFG office on every corner.

I've always had a giant vision, and this company is helping me bring my dreams to fruition. And it's even better than I could have imagined to help others expand their vision and build businesses that will create generations of wealth.

In the near future, this company will dominate the industry. We are going to change millions of lives and we have a unique opportunity to change the future of America.

Eric says, "I'll take the west coast, you take the east coast, and we will meet in the middle."

Why not, right?

Most importantly, helping our leaders get to where they want to go will help us get to where we want to go. It's a beautiful thing and we can all win together.

Chapter 11
Frank Lagattuta

I was the third of four children in a military family. My sister is the oldest, and three boys followed. My dad was the son of Italian immigrants and grew up to become a 20-year serviceman in the Army. He served in both Vietnam and Korea during his tenure. My mom was born in Germany at the end of World War II. Both of my parents were poor growing up, but always made the most of what they had.

The experience of being raised with little by way of luxuries, sometimes without basic necessities, really shaped the attitude they had about anything they achieved and acquired in life. They were conditioned to live lean, so when any abundance arrived, they always approached the abundance with appreciation and gratitude. They also kept the budget tight, as they never knew when the next windfall would occur. This attitude helped frame their perspective on parenting as well. They took pains to make sure that their kids appreciated everything they were able to acquire or achieve.

As a military family with four kids, there was not a great deal of abundance when I was growing up, but we never felt that we were lacking anything. We always had food on the table and clothes to wear. Although we were not as poor as my parents were as kids, we were by no means well off. My parents were masters at making us feel like every other family because they were able to discipline and manage themselves financially with very little.

After 20 years of service, my dad retired from the military as a Lieutenant Colonel and took a job in the private sector starting at $27,000 per year. It was challenging for him to start over with an entry-level job at the age of 44 as his kids were approaching college age.

He was a leader in the military and in life, and rose through the ranks at Xerox. Considering his late start in the private sector, he reached a six-figure income rather quickly. He was always determined to improve his position and once told me that if he could have steak for dinner every Saturday night he would consider himself successful. He achieved this and much more. He was determined and dedicated, worked harder than anyone else around him, and became very successful. I am grateful for the example he set and for the life he gave us growing up.

My mom was a stay-at-home mom. Raising four kids was even more challenging when my dad was deployed for a year or more overseas, especially considering my older brother and I were extremely active. She is a very strong woman with strong values and integrity, an unbelievable work ethic, and a clear view of right and wrong. I believe, often times, she worked harder than my dad did, if that was even possible. That work ethic was instilled in us from an early age. Because of that, my siblings and I share the same attitude about working hard and committing to a goal.

My mom was not all work though. She found times to bring joy and fun to our home, especially as we got older. When my younger brother and I were old enough, she was able to relax a little more and bring her true personality to light. I remember her singing to herself some mornings and laughing about what she was doing. It brought a sense of joy and fun to our home and lives.

Oftentimes, my parents would share some thoughts with us that would help frame our thinking. They lived by these types of ideals, or attitudes, and helped us see the value of them.

Mom's Favorites

"Selbst ist der man." (German phrase that translates to: Self is the man.) Basically meaning, you need to rely on yourself and take responsibility to do things for yourself.

"If trouble finds you, you should not have been there in the first place." I paraphrased a little as there were several versions of this one.

"Laughter is the best medicine."

Dad's Favorites

"Don't let anyone outwork you. Most will quit long before you do, and you will rise because of it."

"If you don't like the rules/plan/vision, do what you have to do to get into a position to make the rules. This will require constant learning, hard work, forward thinking, and paying the price to get there."

"In competition, I hate to lose; losing doesn't feel good to anyone. Accepting losing only makes us mediocre."

"Lead by example! Don't ever ask your people to do something you are not willing to do yourself. This does not mean you have to do everything yourself, but sometimes it sends a powerful message to your people when you roll up your sleeves and dig in."

"When life knocks you down, you get back up – immediately! Don't wallow in your misery, even for a moment. The longer you stay down, the more you are willing to accept the defeat/setback."

"Stay in control and keep a cool head, especially in adversity. Negative emotion can damage relationships and thwart progress towards goals."

"Take care of your people and your people will take care of you."

Those were just a few of the ideals and attitudes that my parents showered on us throughout my childhood and long into my adulthood. Dad always said repetition is the key to learning. I guess that is why he said things over and over again.

My parents came from a tough upbringing, yet found a way to keep us focused on the most important things in life, like family, looking out for each other, working together, sharing responsibility, keeping a positive mental attitude, and maintaining a strong work ethic. My parents always told us how proud they were of us and how much they loved us. This created a mentality of confidence and character within all of their kids. My dad often says he is the richest man in the world based on the family, including kids and grandkids, he and my mom created.

My parents are now 76 and 70 and still say they can outwork anyone. And they do! The foundation they established truly empowered their children to strive to achieve more than they ever achieved. Like every generation before us, the best thing we can do is take the good lessons and leave the bad. As with every parent, we strive to provide a good launching pad for our kids into the world. My parents were no different, and always did what they thought was the right thing for us. They always wanted the best for us. But sometimes, what they thought was best was not always what we wanted our lives to look like.

Security for their children was always paramount. Taking risks was not smart and created unnecessary struggle and uncertainty. Considering this, I went to college, graduated, and started working in the insurance industry for $25,000 a year at a very large insurance company. Growing up, I was taught that if I worked hard, I would work my way up over time, join management, and make a decent living.

During my early years in the industry, I was introduced to a company called World Marketing Alliance (the predecessor of World Financial Group). Due to my security-first upbringing and the perceived security of a W-2 job, I was not willing to seriously consider anything commission-based, and I stayed with my company. During my 10 years of toiling in the employer/employee corporate world and achieving some success, as believed by my parents, I reached a management position and was making about $60,000 per year, plus approximately a $9,000 annual bonus. Yes, you read that right, 10 years later, I was only making $60,000. Stop laughing!

Roughly 10 years later, I was reintroduced to World Financial Group through my wife, who went to a Business Presentation Meeting. She was excited and inspired and told me to come see what she was talking about. During the meeting, I reflected back and thought that it sounded like the same thing I was exposed to with World Marketing Alliance. In many ways it was, but in many ways it was different.

Having been exposed to the financial industry and the challenges of unscrupulous agents, excessive greed, shady sales practices, and facilitating settlements of the numerous class action lawsuits the industry had endured, I realized that I could not get comfortable with a company that did not have a compliance/regulatory division to manage its field force. In my mind, this regulatory role was the biggest difference between WMA and WFG, and the inclusion of the compliance and legal oversight is what made me more comfortable in making the decision to pursue our goals with WFG.

The impetus to seriously consider a commission-based business this time was primarily due to the realization that companies and corporations work hard to maximize the results out of the workforce with as little cost as possible. In other words, they will try to pay as little as someone will accept to perform the functions of the role. That is just good business and sound profit strategy, but it's not always good for the individual. It's especially not good for someone who aspires to achieve greater success in life, like me. This time, I had been in the corporate world and personally experienced how the corporate mentality works. The lucky employees received average annual raises of 3 percent, we were trading time for money, we had to abide by rigid rules and schedules, and we were being micromanaged. These were all things that were counter-intuitive to me as part of my plan for success. It was time for a change.

Dana and I saw WFG as our way to accelerate our success story so we could have the lifestyle others only dream about. During our first year in the business, we made more than our entire combined income from the prior year. Our success story is ongoing, but we have been growing year over year. We've experienced dramatic growth financially, as leaders, as business partners, as parents, and as a married couple, all because WFG has allowed us to regain control of our time and our financial success.

We are creating a legacy for our family for generations to come. Our kids will be great because we are able to create the platform for their launch into their future. Where else can you do this? If there is another place, I have not encountered it.

The Keys to My Personal Success

•   Outwork everyone. I pride myself in working harder and achieving more than others. I do this for no other reason than my personal sense of pride. Maybe it is ego driven. But we all have some sense of ego. Mine might be a little inflated.

- Never quit. I hate quitters. I can't stand someone who gives up when adversity strikes. My heroes are people who face adversity and challenge the odds. I love the underdog who is victorious because of persistence, honesty, ethics, character, and tenacity.
- Stay positive. I always look at the silver lining. The dark cloud serves no one. The silver lining keeps life fun. It inspires us and helps people focus on where they want to go. Bad stuff happens every day. If you don't focus on the positive, bad things will drain your good energy and enthusiasm. There are always positive things to see - if you look for them. I don't let other people bring me problems unless they are also considering the solutions to their problems. Then, and only then, will I give them my ear.
- Never seek or accept mentorship from people who are less successful than you want to be. This is especially true for those who are closest to you. The advice you get from people who have not achieved what you want to achieve, in any capacity, will add little value to you. There are few exceptions to this. While I believe you can learn something from anyone, mentorship should come from those who have succeeded where you have not.
- Learn constantly. Keep developing yourself. Learn something new every day, and talk about those things.
- Laugh every day. Find a reason to laugh several times a day. It feeds the soul.

I am different from others because I am able to stay positive and learn constantly. I believe we are all either moving forward or backward. I have experienced the past. Whether it was good or bad, it is over and I don't want to stay there. The rest of my life is ahead of me.

My Advice to a New Associate

The best advice I can give it to a new associate is to be coachable to those who have succeeded before you. Don't recreate the wheel. You can thrive in our business if you believe in three things.

1.   Believe in the Company. This includes the industry, the crusade, the financial strength, and the leadership.
2.   Believe in the System. Many, not few, have prospered in this company by following the proven system and not modifying it.
3.   Believe in Yourself. You have to believe that you can do whatever it takes to grow through adversity and develop new skills. You can be as successful as you want here; you just have to be willing to pay the price.

My Advice to a Leader Who Is Stuck In a Rut

Go back to basics. The Business Format System is pure and true. The funny thing about a proven system is that it always works. If you hit a plateau or rut, change your associations, go make new friends, recruit some people, field train them, duplicate yourself, and teach them how to duplicate themselves.

Always stay positive and block out negative influences. Leaders need to inspire others to follow. If you are providing value to new business partners and they are inspired by your hard work, success, character, and integrity, they will follow your lead. Be a leader that you would follow and be honest about your strengths and weaknesses. Then build yourself and your skills each day.

Common Mistakes Associates Make

There are a few common mistakes associates make that can derail their growth and success.

1.   Listening to people who are not successful. Listening to someone who has not achieved any real success is like listening to a swim instructor that doesn't know how to swim. Why would you take the risk of getting coaching from

someone who was not successful in what you are trying to learn? Consider your inner circle of mentors. Are they much more successful than you are?

2.   Deviating from the system.   Many people follow the system, as long as it is convenient. Once it gets difficult or uncomfortable, they modify their effort and focus to avoid the discomfort. This only prolongs success or leads to failure.

3.   Lacking belief in self.   Associates often believe they cannot accomplish whatever they want. They bring limiting beliefs into their effort, or lack of effort, because they don't yet have the confidence to pursue their dreams.

Personal Challenges I Had to Overcome

The biggest challenge for me was overcoming the mental impact of resistance from my closest circle - my family and friends. I had to overcome the feeling that I had to prove that our decision to pursue our goals and dreams in WFG was the right choice for us. My brother-in-law was actually the first person, before my siblings or parents, to believe that we would be very successful in this opportunity. He was also the first to listen with an open ear to what the company was all about and what we wanted to achieve here. And, he was actually the first to refer a friend to our business. I am grateful for his support and encouragement. Because I respected his opinion and because we have been mutually supportive of each other's growth over the years, this gesture of trust and confidence has played a big part in overcoming my concern for what others thought about us or the business.

The other major challenge I had to overcome was reaching the understanding that, as a spouse/partner, my wife's challenges were also my challenges. We had to work together to reinforce, encourage, and support each other through both of our personal challenges. When Dana was going through personal adversity, I would always try to direct her to focus on the silver lining so she could push towards something positive. In some heated moments of frustration, she would often say I was delusional because I was not letting her focus on the adversity she was facing. We laugh about those moments now, but it was difficult to change Dana's vision when she was on a mental death spiral. Just remember, when you are married, you share each other's struggles and challenges. There is no one better than your spouse to help you get through the adversity and back on track.

Things I Would Do Differently If I Had To Start Over

If I had to start over, I would be more coachable from the beginning. There is real value in putting your head down and just going to work. Also, I would have primarily focused on being the example more and helping the team grow in their success sooner. Helping people achieve success only adds to your success and impact as a leader. As my dad always said, "Take care of your people and your people will take care of you."

My Vision for the Future of My Business

Dana and I have a deep desire to be in top leadership for WFG. We believe strongly in the crusade and fully expect our reach and impact to expand globally. I see us on the Presidents Council for WFG in future years. I also see our business consistently developing new leaders and strong, ethical, enduring, profitable agencies under our mentorship.

Besides the security, lifestyle, and legacy that we want for our family for generations to come, we also want to pursue philanthropic endeavors to raise up communities around us. I am an advocate of helping people by teaching them to help themselves. The incentives we provide through our assistance should move people to become self-sufficient. I believe we can positively affect future generations by projecting honesty, integrity, and value to all who will have it.

Chapter 12
Dana Lagattuta

When I reflect on my childhood and my experiences, I am filled with gratitude. Life was not always easy, but experiences are the best opportunities for growth because the test comes before the lesson. Therefore, I took the lesson a lot more seriously.

I have very fond memories of sharing holiday dinners and birthday parties with my extended family. I remember running around my grandparents' gigantic home with my cousins, swimming in the pool, playing football or Frisbee in the cul-de-sac, laughing, and having fun.

I was especially fortunate to be close to my grandparents growing up. They were local and very involved in my life. My grandfather worked hard, running and investing in businesses, and was financially savvy. He and my grandmother raised four sons, including my father, built a beautiful home, enjoyed a dream retirement, and were married for 50 years. Because I had their example, I always knew I would make my way into that lifestyle.

I was blessed to have two great parents who loved me and taught me a lot about fighting hard for your goals. They got married when they were very young, and divorced when I was only two years old. Later, they both remarried. My mom and stepdad made good money, but he was a gambler and, ultimately, gambled everything away, including our home. For me, that lack of stability produced a lot of fear and anxiety.

When I was 11 years old, my mom got Crohn's disease. She had to have about 15 surgeries and she couldn't work. That came around the same time that she was splitting from her husband. I can remember that time as being the most difficult in my life up to that point.

The divorces and the health issues caused a lot of stress, but mostly caused financial burden that was almost debilitating. When I was old enough, I started working to help pay the bills. I was always glad to help and never felt cheated in doing so. I believe that early responsibility helped me develop a sense of reality and work ethic. It also offered me a very healthy perspective. I remember thinking on many occasions, even in my younger years, that I could make things better for my mom and myself. I felt I had the control to improve our lifestyle, and I was naïve enough to believe that. Therefore, I went to work on that goal.

I also remember thinking that things would be different for me when I got married and had kids. My mother later married a man who she is married to today. He is a wonderful, supportive, and down-to-earth man who has enriched our lives so much. My mother has immense strength and has overcome so much adversity, both financially and medically, I admire her so much and I have drawn so much strength from her.

My father went through his own ups and downs and battled many demons, as we all have. Yet, he was present, he always attended my sports events and dance recitals, and I never remember him missing a weekend. Unfortunately, he couldn't provide a stable environment for me during this time in my life. He later settled down and remarried a woman who has also enriched our lives. She and my father had a wonderful daughter, my half-sister, who was born when I was 16 years old. That was one of the major blessings in my life. My father became a Christian late in life and began to introduce me to having faith and belief in the Lord.

As our lives began to settle, things became clearer. Looking back, I can connect the dots. Steve Jobs said, "You can't connect the dots looking forward, only looking back. You have to trust that the dots will connect somehow." By having that faith, it gives you the strength to take chances and the wisdom to keep adversity in its proper place.

Our experiences offer great opportunities for growth and change. Without them, we are very limited in who we can become and what we can offer the world. I believe that God blessed me when he gave me such great moments and memories. I also believe he blessed me through the times of struggle and turmoil. Without having experienced both, I would never appreciate what it means to have a great life. It's been a process. Early in my life, I somehow understood that we're all products of our environment, but we don't have to be victims of our circumstances.

It started when, for the first time ever, I really wanted something and was inspired to go after it, but realized that my current habits were not going to get me there. That was the first acknowledgement that I needed to grow. It happened when I came into this business and saw what was possible. I wanted the lifestyle, and income, and family environment, and flexible schedule. But, I really didn't completely get all that at first. I just wanted success.

Straight out of college, I was hired to work for a very large and reputable company that was handling a class action lawsuit in its life insurance division. They hired thousands of people through a temp agency, and they were paying us all hourly and offering overtime. I was making really good money and I knew exactly how many hours of overtime I needed to work to double my income. However, they must have seen it as good work ethic, because I was promoted to middle level manager. I was excited for the opportunity and they switched me from an hourly wage to a salary. I later realized that meant no overtime.

Regardless, my job was to look at each individual complaint and all the available evidence and, if appropriate, offer a monetary award. Through that job, I started to develop pride in my work and to grow personally. I was around many people who were older than me who were shooting for something in life. One of those people was Frank, who became one of my mentors. He wasn't my direct boss, but was somebody I looked up to. Most managers just cared about the bottom line, especially at that time when things were volatile and the company was looking to cut back after paying millions of dollars in class action claims. But I could see instantly that Frank had rock-solid integrity and always did the right thing. I gravitated to him and learned from him. We were friends for a long time before the relationship deepened romantically. We then got married and began our lives together.

During that time, I saw the ugly side of the insurance industry, including forgery, misleading clients, and omission of critical information. It was all there. The years I spent studying the experiences of some of the millions of families who had participated in this lawsuit had a big impact on me. I saw people who felt misled and confused. They were unsure of where their money was going or whether the products they had been sold would deliver.

The company ended up paying back its customers and making them whole and went on to become one of the most highly-respected firms in the industry. I didn't know that experience would end up fueling a passion for a business that I would later be introduced to. Again, you can't connect the dots looking ahead, only looking back.

As we were wrapping up the lawsuit, the company began to go public through a demutualization process, and Frank and I knew our jobs would be coming to an end. That's when I started doing mortgages on a part-time basis. When I asked a very good friend for referrals to realtors and financial advisors, she handed me a card from someone she knew at World Financial Group. I called him repeatedly, but he was inactive at the time and never responded. At some point, he went to a convention with the company and came back excited and rejuvenated and finally called me back. I told him what I was doing, and he said I needed to come meet with his colleague, Jaime Villalovos. I went there prepared to ask the agents to refer me their clients, but I didn't get a word in. Jaime presented the business to me, and that was that. I was sold on the company within an hour.

The Keys to My Personal Success

Before I began my official training as an associate, I attended an orientation where one of the senior managers shared the story of the company. I fell in love with the business right there, and I remember two very specific things that night that shaped my future in this industry forever.

First was the mission. I was impressed with the information and the passion with which it was delivered. I came to recognize the company's crusade to educate families and businesses in our communities and help them become stronger financially.

Second was the transparency. Considering my previous six years in the industry, working to correct an injustice, it was refreshing and, quite frankly, shocking to see what was being shared in that room. With potential clients and potential associates sitting together, the presenter enthusiastically disclosed the income earned by agents for helping people save money and protect their families. This would have been unheard of, both at my previous company and also in the mortgage business where I had been working. So, to observe that level of transparency solidified my commitment to the business and deepened my faith to move forward with full conviction.

I found a reason to fully commit and engage. I knew it wouldn't be easy; however, the unknown didn't stop me from moving forward. While the known adversity may have stopped me in my tracks a few times, commitment kept me moving forward. Commitment is the foundation of anything worth having. We need to have commitment to our marriages, our families, our relationships, our children, and our passions.

When my husband makes a decision, he makes a firm commitment. He proved this when he married me and when we decided to partner together in business. No matter what is thrown our way, the commitment is what he is honoring. I have learned that when I make a commitment, it is because it is important to me. There should be nothing external, including other people's opinions or any adversity, that should change that.

Unfortunately, I didn't have that same quality before I met my husband. Commitment to me meant doing something until it became difficult. That was something that needed to change for me right away if I was going to be significant. Having the resolve to know you are on the right path and further commit to that path is what minimizes unnecessary distractions. Continuously questioning the path creates many distractions. A major key to my success in my marriage, my business and in my faith is my increasing commitment level to these areas of my life.

The second principal I believe is necessary to be successful in anything is coachability. This is described as moving at the speed in which the instruction is given. Coming into the business, I did not have any experience in business, sales, or leadership. So, I submitted to following instructions from those who did have experience in those areas. I did not have much past success, so my ego didn't get in the way of my progress. I was too naïve to be skeptical and, as a result, put my head down and worked the system. I was a clean slate and a sponge, and that was a huge advantage for me.

My Advice to a New Associate

Many people I see come into the business sabotage the chance of success through two major pitfalls.

1.   The first pitfall in this business is skepticism. Skepticism creates paralysis and robs us of all future value. I have shared a 30-plus year friendship with a girl from my elementary school. She met a man in high school and told me, "I will marry that man." She fell head-over-heels in love with him and, years later, they were engaged to be married. Three weeks before they were going to be married, she found out he had been cheating on her and was involved in many different relationships over the years. The wedding was called off and my friend was devastated. After months of depression, therapy, and prayer, she was able to rebuild her life and move forward. She found a new career, new friends, and afew years later, found another boyfriend. This man was kind and loyal and, while not perfect, he is not a cheater. Furthermore, he has never given her any reason to doubt his commitment to their relationship and he has always been honest and forthcoming.

However, my girlfriend still doesn't trust him and is paranoid in the relationship. She checks his phone for inappropriate text messages when he is sleeping, she tries to access his email account when he steps away from his computer, and she is filled with fear and anxiety every time he is with friends or working late. Needless to say, the relationship ended because she assumed that because one relationship went south, that every relationship would also fail. From my current perspective, that is just absurd. Does one bad apple ruin the bunch? Does one pushy and insincere car salesman who doesn't have your best interest at heart mean every automobile representative is the same way? Does one difficult day mean every other day will be just as difficult? No! Skepticism is created from past experiences, or the past experiences of other people. Usually, those experiences have nothing to do with the situation at hand. Yet, we allow that skepticism to cripple us and hold us back from our true potential and development. Skepticism breeds fear and hesitation, and hesitation and fear create inaction, and inaction creates failure.

2.   The second major pitfall in this business is arrogance. Past success in any business or field is a valuable asset to have when coming into this business. Higher education is also valued at our firm. However, past success and education don't guarantee success in our business. In order to learn the system of our business, new associates need mentorship, training, and coaching.

Sometimes, new agents have the mentality that they want to do things their way because they have been successful before and they have great ideas. What they don't recognize is that a system is far more effective than ideas. Just as the rock of discipline, or what we do, is far more effective than the shifting wind of emotion or how we feel. Commit to relying on the system while simultaneously using your past achievements and successes to enhance your success. The system is the key.

The two pitfalls I described above are detrimental to a career in WFG because they don't allow for coachability. Moving at the speed of the instruction requires listening to the person giving the instruction. There is a level of submission involved, and many people I have seen struggle with that for many reasons. Remember, you are not submitting to a person, but to a system that has been proven over and over again and has changed thousands of lives and has paid us millions and millions of dollars.

Learning to trust my mentors, Jaime and Shawn Villalovos, made it easier to be coachable. Like any relationship, time and experience are important in building that trust. They asked me to do things I didn't understand, like introduce them to my market and invest a lot of time in the business through Saturday trainings, boot camps, events, Elite Circle classes, and more. But, I made the decision early on that I was going to take the leap of faith, and if I messed up, at least I tried. That was huge. If I had hesitated, I would have been like everybody else who waits for the green light or the guarantee that they are never going to get hurt and the business is guaranteed to work. Holding back won't to lead to success. When fear is low and faith is high, clarity is revealed. I began to see that my mentors had a vested interest in my success. Our leadership wants us to win because it's in their best financial interest. I am so grateful to my mentors and partners in the business, as I am a product of all of them. The support system we have shared as a team has been the most important aspect of this environment. Everyone wants to be a part of something. In WFG, you are a part something much larger than yourself.

These learned traits served me well, and I would recommend that any new agent in our company try to develop them and turn them into habits. There is a benefit in following the desire to improve yourself, having the willingness to take a leap of faith, being ready to accept coaching, and committing to your goals and choices.

I would say the most important element of building a solid foundation in this business is for a new associate to know why they are working the business. When you think of all the things that can drive somebody out of the business - the negativity, the scenario of disaster, the perceived rejection we all face - none of it matters if you're clear on where you're going. Those things are all small when related to the type of lifestyle you will experience if you put in the time and effort.

Perhaps some respond more effectively to considering the alternative to reaching their goals in this business. Without the opportunity to accomplish goals for your family, what would life look like? When I looked seriously at the alternative to me working hard in this business, when it came to my family, it was not something I was willing to accept or tolerate.

My winning in the business meant freedom for my mother. Without that, she would be told by an employer to come to work in spite of her medical condition and regardless of what would be required to keep her healthy. That was a matter of life or death as far as I was concerned. For my mother, my kids, and my family, we will create our path. We will decide what is in our best interest.

My husband and I decided we wanted to be the example for our children to follow, and not leave that to someone who makes a larger statement through being more successful. That would mean that someone else had more courage than their parents and that someone else was willing to rely on faith while we were held back by fear. When there is a lack of clarity, or the goal is just money, then the adversary continues to attack the weakness. The adversity then appears bigger and bigger and, ultimately, is the anchor that keeps us down.

Nobody will ever have a shot at winning in the business long term, nor will they have the endurance to do so, if they're not completely clear on why they're doing it. It takes a while for most people to achieve the clarity they need. They have to dig deeper than what might be comfortable to figure out what they want or what they don't want. Initially, when people come into the business, it's difficult to see past their current circumstances. It's hard to see the forest through the trees. That doesn't mean the forest isn't there, or that we won't arrive there. Identifying your true purpose has a lot to do with being introspective and asking yourself tough questions, such as: What do I want my life to be about? What do I want my legacy to be? What kind of lifestyle do I want for my family? What does my ideal life look like? And what am I willing to give up to have this lifestyle?

My Advice to a Leader Who Is Stuck In a Rut

I believe a rut is simply a disconnect with our whys. To get out of a rut, it's important to reconnect with your true heart's desire or to reassess what that might be. The renewed energy and enthusiasm of envisioning your lifestyle and knowing you have access to the business and the system to achieve your heart's desire will rid you of your rut.

Believe it or not, a rut is created in life as a result of our energy level and focus. When we are excited about life, we create momentum. John Maxwell refers to this as "The Law of The Big Mo." Momentum is a very powerful source and can move your business further then you might realize at this point in your career. The willingness to put in the effort and work upfront to get a clear image of your outcome will minimize a rut. The clarity of purpose and renewed energy will bring a wow factor that will draw high-caliber people to your life and to your business.

Common Mistakes Associates Make

WFG is the greatest part time opportunity in the United States of America. Where else can you maintain the predictability of an income, have control of your own schedule, have the power to protect your priorities of faith and family, and learn a very regulated and profitable business? Do you know of another business that has the potential to pay an associate more than what they are earning at their full-time job by only working part-time hours? This business provides people with an opportunity to walk away from a job they hate and not to be held hostage to a paycheck. The part time opportunity provides a sense of security for families as they can learn this business without focusing on the money. Of course, money is necessary in our business. But when we focus on money alone, it's difficult to earn. However, when we focus on learning new skills, developing ourselves, and remaining focused on the crusade of our company, the money comes in abundance.

While the opportunity is certainly great, one mistake I see too often is when associates prematurely making the decision to work WFG on a full-time basis. The thought alone can be a distraction. Don't assume that just because someone now has more time on their hands that they will be productive. Going full time too soon can lead to financial problems. Many times, we see the financial stress overwhelm people, and their vision is lost, and the crusade is lost because they're focusing on the now. In this business, you just have to keep investing and planting seeds. The harvest will come with time.

Another pitfall I see is the delusion of what activities produce income in the business. There are actions that drive income almost immediately, such as being in an appointment, sharing the story of our company, or being on the phone to schedule more appointments. Those actions are called "green time." Then, there is the busy work, such as paperwork, preparation for BPMs, checking emails, and other general tasks. If the line is not clearly drawn as to what the work of the business really is, then we begin to play tricks on ourselves.

There was a gentleman in our agency who was considered a full time agent. His full time status was more related to his lack of another job as opposed to actually earning a full time income. He spent time in the office four to five days a week, but didn't have activity to take up the hours he was "working" in the business. He attended the BPMs on Tuesday nights and Saturday mornings. He would be the first to arrive and last to leave, and he was a team player for sure. One day, his wife called me and expressed some concerns. She said, "I don't get it, he is working so hard. He leaves the house at 9 a.m. and on Tuesday night doesn't get home until midnight. Anyone who works that hard should be cash-flowing, right?" What I had to explain to her was that her husband didn't clock in or clock out and we don't get paid for being in the office. I also had to explain to her that BPM attendance has its value, but it doesn't create income. In fact, the BPM finishes around 9 p.m., not midnight. Sometimes we have a locker room talk with our licensed agents, but, even with that, we go until maybe 10 p.m. What we realized, was that he was going to eat dinner after the BPM with his colleagues. Once his wife found out that he wasn't working the way she thought he was on Tuesday nights, she was frustrated, but it made sense to her. The epiphany was that her husband's lack of results had nothing to do with the business, but more to do with the husband's lack of winning habits.

Personal Challenges I Had to Overcome

I feel very blessed to have the parents I had in my life. They loved me and supported me in everything I did. In hindsight, other than the difficulties that came with divorce and illness, I don't recall being exposed to any real personal adversity. Perhaps the support system around me - my parents, grandparents, and some other influences in my life - shielded me from any further hardship.

I struggled with a weak mindset coming into the business. For some reason, I wasn't prepared to handle the difficulty of the process. When you want to do something bigger than the average, adversity is going to come, and I was ill-prepared to handle this type of struggle. My biggest challenge was being what we refer to as a pansy. I lacked skill in how to process some of the frustrations that came with building a business. It created some negative feelings of stress, anxiety, lack of belief, and wanting to take the path of least resistance. Fortunately, I am blessed to have a husband who is strong and loyal and believes in commitment. When he and I made the decision to move forward in this business, like everything else in his life, he had made a commitment to endure until the goal was achieved. Other people's opinions on our decisions, or how much adversity we encountered on the way to achieving our goal, did not change the direction we were going.

My decision to move forward in the business did not come from such conviction. Originally, I was committed until it became difficult. Clearly, that wasn't a conscious choice. That was simply how I approached most things in my life at that time. I'll admit, I did contemplate quitting on multiple occasions as a reaction to the negative emotions that I couldn't control. Fortunately, my husband would not contemplate quitting. Having a strong and supportive spouse is important in all areas of our life, including this business. The days I came home having those negative feelings, Frank was the recipient of my venting and frustration. I am so grateful that my husband was strong enough to believe in me and in the business so that he could respond to my early years of frustration in a way that encouraged me. At my weakest point, had my husband gave me any opportunity for an "out," I may not be writing this chapter right now. He didn't let me off the hook. In fact, he encouraged me and reminded me of all the reasons I can and should continue to work the business.

That is a very critical part of the story. If I had not been encouraged to stay in the business, I would never have had the opportunity to grow and develop the tools to handle the adversity that came our way. I developed the skills and mindset to tackle any of the issues that caused negative feelings in the past. Whether it is a healthy perspective, being clear on my vision and my whys, or having strong leadership skills, all of it has been part of my development process through this business.

My leadership and mentors, my associations, the successes this company affords, the integrity of the system and leadership, and the team that inspires me every day to push forward, have all been instrumental in getting me to this point. I often ponder what life would look like if I had given into the weakness early on. The quality of life this company has afforded our family is unlike anything we would ever experience in any other work environment. I have been able to put my family first in so many ways. I have stayed home with my children. Now that they are older, I have the flexibility to spend time volunteering at their school. I can take days off with them during the summer to have fun experiences. I can step in to help financially with family members as needed. And most recently, I was able to spend every day with my father as he was dying in the hospital. During that difficult time, I was able to be at the hospital every time he came out of sedation so that he could see my face. I was able to be there until he took his last breath. This was another reinforcement that the struggles and sacrifices made early on were not only worth it, but small in comparison.

The toughest battles are from within. During those times, self-awareness and assessment is critical to growing out of that to reach a new level. I remember a turning point in my business. I came home frustrated after having a rough day and I was getting ready to unload on Frank, which was a bad habit I had gotten into. But on this one night, I was about 15 minutes away from home, and I remember just thinking, "You know what, I need to get myself right before I go into that house. I can't keep relying on Frank to talk me out of quitting; I need to learn to do it on my own." I knew at that point I wasn't quitting this business. I had no intention of doing so. I was giving into my weakness and, at some point, taking Frank's strength for granted. I decided that when I got home we would talk about whatever good stuff had happened that day and why I was committed to doing this business. That was a shift for me and, thereafter, I was never the same. I certainly had battles and adversity, but they were all within my control

Things I Would Do Differently If I Had To Start Over

If I could start over, the main thing I would do differently would be going wider faster. Whatever success I have now in the business is based on my width. Had I doubled that, I would now be probably quadruple the size. I'm focusing on that now, but it's taken me 11 years to finally make that commitment because I got lazy. When you develop an organization that is self-running and, in many ways, stronger than the leader is, there is a risk of becoming stagnant. There are a few areas we can never become stagnant in and we must always keep growing in these areas. Those include direct recruiting, developing ourselves, and staying economically disciplined.

Also, I would have been more coachable later in my business. I was very coachable in the beginning, but the higher up we go in the company and the more success we have, we sometimes tend to lose that commitment to absolute coachability. I've always tried to check that and regroup, and I think I'm better than most. But, there have been moments in my career when I didn't listen and I didn't embrace the coaching the way I could have. If I had, I'd be in a different place.

My Vision for the Future of My Business

I was told when I first came into the business that this was a company of destiny, and we would do great things, and we were controversial, but we were only going to get bigger and grow more powerful as time went by. All those things have come true. So looking another 10 years into the future, I see this company becoming the biggest broker-dealer in the country, having the most licensed agents, having a tremendous, positive economic impact on middle America, and making a huge difference.

When we were in Costa Rica in October of 2014, somebody asked our company president and CEO, Joe DiPaola, about his vision for the future. He said, "I can't have a vision for the future, because I have to be flexible and able to adapt and adjust to shape this company the way you want it to be. Your vision has to be my vision."

That was eye-opening for me, because I realized that we can take this company wherever we want to. I had been told that before, but I believe it more and more the higher I get in leadership.

Our Freedom Builders organization is going to do great things and become a well-known brand throughout the country. We are committed to producing hundreds of seven-figure earners. The impact we can make with the proper influence is exciting to us and we are moving in that direction. What we do for people in the community is powerful and it transcends the financial principals we teach. It allows families and marriages the chance to have their finances be a positive aspect of their life rather than a negative. The knowledge we deliver that causes people to save money builds confidence, and confidence allows people to achieve more than they thought possible. Our associates are encouraged and praised and recognized for their efforts. We see the best in our teammates and offer them a platform to be the best they can be or choose to be.

We parade our agents across stages in arenas that major leaders of the world have walked across and presented on, because the work we do daily is making a major impact on the world. You can't see this from the outside, and you won't see the power from the spectator's seats. To see the power of our company and to enjoy the blessings it offers, you must get in the game and play. Sometimes, you will win and sometimes you will lose. At times, you will make that buzzer shot and succeed. Other times, you will miss. However, if you stay in the game, you will win the ultimate game of having quality of life in ways most people will never experience.

I am grateful to this company, to my leadership, to the team, to my husband, and, most of all, to my children. Our future is bright and success is imminent for those who wage the war on mediocrity with us. It is more worth it than you ever thought it would be.

CHAPTER 12
DANA LAGATTUTA

Chapter 13
Veronica Jaime

I was born and raised in San Jose, California, by two hard-working parents who came from El Salvador at a young age. I'm the eldest of three and the only girl. I remember seeing my parents work two jobs since I was small until about age 16 so that my brothers and I could live in a good community with good schools. I appreciate them showing me hard work, determination, and sacrifice. They always spoke to us about the importance of savings. Living in south San Jose in a four-bedroom home meant my parents had to rent two rooms to afford the mortgage.

At age 15, I began to work. I remember having to take the city bus to get to and from work since my parents had such a busy schedule. One day, I was riding the bus and, as I got home, I began to cry out of frustration of how I wish things could be easier and different. My mom reminded me that nothing comes easy and you have to work hard for what you want. She proceeded to tell me and show me what she had accomplished with an opportunity and hard work. She made sure to tell me every day how important it was to attend college and get a good job with benefits.

Over the next few years, I graduated high school, attended a four-year university, and managed to get a job at the university. It was there that I meet my wonderful and charming husband, Juan Jaime, who I married a few years later. After a few administrative jobs and serving as a domestic violence advocate, I found myself achieving all that I was told to do since I was little. I was hired to work as a state employee for the Santa Clara County Superior Court.

I've always been a worrier and a reserved person while Juan has been the dreamer, doer, and all-in type of guy. Juan and I purchased our first home at the young age of 23. It was definitely a scary moment for me, being that we were young and could barely afford it. But, Juan said we could do it, so we went for it. I had a great job at the time and Juan had just graduated college, but could not find a job and ended up working for his dad.

I was introduced to the business through a Top 25 list, which led to a KTP appointment at my friend's house. I was not interested, but I referred Juan instead, since he was working with his dad in plumbing and I knew he was looking for something better. The following week, Juan attended a Tuesday night BPM. I just remember him coming home excited, saying he had started a business with WFG and he was going to be successful. Imagine what I was thinking! I did not know much of the company, or what they did, but I believed in Juan. I had seen the obstacles he had to overcome to be where he was already. He had a no quitting mentality when he did something.

Our WFG journey began in 2004. We jumped through many hurdles, went through our share of adversity, and had an unsupportive circle. But, through it all, we never quit.

I would not change anything, because it's made me stronger. It has helped me grow and be the women I am today – a leader. Now, I am a successful business women, a mother of two, and a Latina CEO at the age of 32. Who says you can't have it all? You just have to be willing to do what others are not willing to.

The Keys to My Personal Success

I describe the keys to my personal success as being a good listener, making others feel important, falling in love with the business, and seeing myself as Juan's co-pilot in our business We are both equally important, but focus on different areas. I came to our business full time at the end of 2011. As the co-pilot, I am able to be the extra eyes and ears to our business. I help Juan alleviate the many hats he had to wear when he was running the business alone. I focus on the operations side of our business and guiding my frontline leadership group, while Juan focuses on the field and duplicating himself. Juan and I went from SMD to EVC and from $100,000 to crossing over $650,000 in income.

My Advice to a New Associate

My advice to a new associate would be to treat this business like a business! This is not a 9 to 5 job. You have to have a schedule, whether you're part time or full time, and make sure you tell your family so they know what to expect.

You also need to have clear reasons why you are doing this business, and set a deadline. Juan had been in the business for five years before we decided to make a plan for me to come on board full time. It took five years because we never set a deadline or mapped out how we would get there. Remember, "A goal without a deadline is just a dream."

My Advice to a Leader Who Is Stuck In a Rut

My advice to a leader who is stuck in a rut is to seek mentorship within the business. Find someone who can relate to what you're going through and help you get back on track. I've noticed that when we are faced with adversity or hit a bump on the road to success, and we don't have positive people surrounding us, the negative or doubtful people will come in at the right time and pull us from what we once felt was our vehicle to success.

Common Mistakes Associates Make

One of the most common mistakes I've seen associates make is thinking they need to reinvent the wheel. The key to duplication and growing in this business is keeping things simple so that others can follow your lead and feel they can do it too.

The second mistake I've seen associates make is holding onto the wrong associations. You should surround yourself with people who make you feel uncomfortable and push you beyond your limits. Find others who have a big vision and keep you motivated. Ask yourself, how am I being influenced?

Personal Challenges I Had to Overcome

One of my biggest challenges in our business was myself. I cared too much about what others would say if I left a good-paying career with benefits. I started to ask a lot of "what if" questions. What if I failed? What if they are right? I cared about other people's opinions so much that it took me five years to leave my career and make the transition to join Juan in our business.

As a spouse, we sometimes say it's "their business" instead of "our business." For the first five years, that is exactly how I felt. I let it be his business and not ours. I was not involved or around the winning environment of the office. I believed that supporting from home was enough. Later, however, I came to find out it was not. When building a business, you invest in it physically and emotionally and you give it your all. That is what Juan was doing. He was being coachable to Eric Olson. With that, Juan started missing family functions, birthday parties, and BBQ's. Instead, he was always at the office training or out in the field. I let others make me feel like a single mom because, in corporate America, "normal" is translated as a Monday through Friday job from 7 a.m. to 5 p.m.

As time passed, I began to feel distant from Juan and I was forgetting the reasons why he had started the business. I no longer felt like he was doing it for us and I began to question our marriage and, for the first and only time, I asked Juan to quit the business to get a full-time job or I would separate from him. Thank God Juan was not having either one. He said, "We are in this marriage until the end and we are doing this business because I am not a quitter." A year later, at a convention, Juan and I decided to make this our business. I began to attend business meeting, trainings, and big events. Just by being present, I began feeling like I was part of the business. We took action, mapped out how I would join the business full time, understood what it would take, and created a deadline. On December 2011, I went full time.

Things I Would Do Differently If I Had To Start Over

God has a plan, and it's all about timing. But, if I had to start over, I would have mapped and created a deadline to go full time sooner. I saw how important our teamwork at home was and it only became stronger when we decided to both work towards one goal. The teamwork makes the dream work that much faster.

My Vision for the Future of My Business

Part of my dream is to see my team, Diamond Leadership Development, winning not just for themselves, but for their families. To have their kids call them their heroes, just like my eight-year-old does now. I see our company dominating the industry and I want to continue to be part of the growth and success.

I would like to end by saying "thank you" to Jeff and Cam Levitan for making this possible and being a great example to us and many.

Chapter 14
Juan Jaime

I was born in Leon Guanajuato, Mexico, and came to the United States at the age of 14. I am the middle of three kids, with an older and a younger sister. My parents brought me to California for a better opportunity in life. We struggled financially when my whole family came to San Jose, California. We constantly moved due to our financial situation and I attended seven high schools during my four years. I still managed to graduate with good grades and, as a result, received a scholarship to attend a private, four-year university.

During my four years in college, life wasn't easy, especially financially since my parents never saved money for me to attend college. I had to have multiple part time jobs to make it through. It was during that time that I met my beautiful wife, Veronica. I graduated with honors and a major in business administration.

The Keys to My Personal Success

A year after graduation, one of Veronica's friends invited me to attend a corporate overview in one of the San Jose offices. At that time, I was working in plumbing with my dad since I couldn't find a good job after graduation. My dad gave me the opportunity to work with him, but every day he used to tell me, "Juan, I don't want you to end up like me. Look for something better; you were born to do something great with your life." So when WFG came into my life, I took the opportunity from day one. That Tuesday night, I meet Eric Olson and my career started.

My Advice to a New Associate

My advice to a new associate would be to believe they can win big here in WFG. The difference between people making a million or more and the ones that don't is their habits - good or bad. I recommend surrounding yourself with positive people who want to see you win. It is hard to come into this business and expect big results without changing your associations. One thing I did really well was staying around leaders and examples of success to the point that I started believing I could win too. They say you become who you hang out with. So, as a new associate you have to be very aware of your associations. My mentor advised me early in my career, "Change your friends or change your friends." That made all the difference in the world. I recommend that new associates do the same.

My Advice to a Leader Who Is Stuck In a Rut

When I first stated in WFG at the age of 23, I achieved success pretty quickly. In the first eight months, I got my Senior Marketing Director promotion. I earned my $100,000 dollar ring in the first 12 months of my career. At that time, Veronica was working at the Santa Clara County Superior Court and had a decent position making almost a six-figure income. Our combined incomes were around $200,000 dollars. That was more money than we had ever made before.

I got pretty comfortable with that income, especially because neither of us came from money. I stayed like that for about five years, but it got to the point that I wanted more. I had no momentum, but I knew I wanted to compete and get my wife full time with me. So we committed 100% to run CEO club numbers and it transformed my business. If any leader is in the same situation where the business is not where you want, look at yourself in the mirror and make a decision to change. Change starts with the leader. The speed of the leader determines the speed of the pack.

Common Mistakes Associates Make

One of the biggest mistakes I see associates make is overcomplicating things. This business is pretty simple. It's not always easy, but it is simple. One of the strengths of our company is our system. But people still don't follow it. I remember hearing people at the office say, "Don't reinvent the wheel." All you have to do is keep it simple.

Other mistakes I have seen associates make is stopping the activities that helped them reach success. Our system is recruit, fast start, and field train. I have often watched associates get a recruit and stop to manage their team. Instead, they should focus on getting more recruits and continuing to run the system.

Last but not least, a lot of people focus on sales instead of building agencies. World Financial Group is a Financial marketing company with a great platform to create outlets. Sales don't create outlets, but recruits do. Don't confuse the two.

Personal Challenges I Had to Overcome

When I first got started, I had to fully understand who was going to support me in my new business venture. I thought that since going from plumbing to a business man in the financial industry was a good change for me, that all of my friends and family were going to be super supportive. But the reality was very different. My mom and dad were always supportive and they always told me to keep going, even when times were tough. My in-laws were, and still are, very instrumental to my success. I couldn't ask for better in-laws. They always go out of their way to help me and Veronica to make sure our business is running strong. The first time I went to the national convention as a new agent, my mother-in-law let me borrow money to buy my ticket.

I invited all of my friends to come to see my business, hoping they would join me and we could build it together. But out of the ten that went, not one of them joined. That didn't stop me from continuing to go forward. I wanted to prove to them that the business was good. A lot of them told me, "Once you are making money, we will join you." If you currently get that from your family and friends, I'm sorry to tell you, but they won't join you even when you making it big - at least most wont.

I used all of the negativity and disappointments from my loved ones to fuel me up with the desire to prove them wrong. At the end of the day, I just knew that becoming successful was not for everyone. You have to be careful who you listen to, especially when it comes to business advice. As long as you know why you are doing this, that's all that matters. For me, my reasons why are my family, Veronica, and my two beautiful boys - Jacob and Christopher.

Things I Would Do Differently If I Had To Start Over

If I were to start this business all over again, I would have focused more on recruiting from day one. Our system is created to build distribution channels. I didn't fall in love with recruiting until about four years ago, and that's when my business transformed. I went from SMD to EVC in less than three years. But the first six years, when recruiting was not my focus, I was stuck as a small SMD.

I would also put more of a focus on personal development. You can't effectively lead people if you are not constantly growing yourself. Leading a large organization is very rewarding, especially when you see your teammates lives changing in front of your eyes all because of a decision you made. We are in the business of people. To move a large amount of people, you have to become a master at human nature. One of my great mentors, Greg Kapp, always says, "Products always change, but people are always people." A mistake I made early on was focusing too much on the products instead of the people. When I made that shift, my business changed and I started attracting leaders into my organization.

My Vision for the Future of My Business

Now, going into my ten year anniversary in WFG, I'm so excited of what is yet to come. I have never seen the momentum that the company has right now. We need to keep moving at the same speed to take full advantage of these special times. I know that WFG is going to be the leading company in North American financial services. More importantly, we are helping to create financially independent families. My team and I are working very hard to be one of the big contributors and dominant teams in all of WFG. My vision is to show people that you can have a well-rounded life of faith, family, finance, fitness, and fun, all while winning in this business.

There are no shortcuts to success. The only time success comes before work is in the dictionary. My wife and I are blessed to be given this opportunity to change our last name forever, and know we have the responsibility to do the same for others. Don't give up! As long as you don't quit, you still have a chance.

Conclusion

YOU CAN DO THIS! Every time you hear a success story at a convention, at church, read it in a book, or watch it in a movie; know that its purpose is to inspire you to take massive action and pursue your dreams. You can have more, do more, and be more. All it takes is more effort and more persistence. *Rise of the Next Wave* is more than just another book of stories and lessons. It's a reminder that there is another opportunity after this wave, to be a part of and lead the next wave. Good luck on your personal journey, may it be fulfilling every step of the way!

Jeff Levitan

Disclaimer & Copyright Page

Disclaimer

Published by: Empower Media, Inc.